Computing Research

&

Innovation

(CRINN)

Vol 1

November 2016

Computer Sciences

Mathematical Sciences

Computer Network & Data Communications

Information Technology & System Sciences

By:

Faculty of Computer & Mathematical Sciences

Universiti Teknologi MARA

Perlis Branch, Malaysia

http://crinn.conferencehunter.com/openconf.php

Editorial Committee

Editor-in-Chief

Mahfudzah Othman

Panel Editors:

Aznoora Osman (Dr.)

Nadia Abdul Wahab (Dr.)

Shukor Sanim Mohd Fauzi (Dr.)

Mohd Nizam Osman

Hawa Mohd Ekhsan

Mohammad Hafiz Ismail

Alif Faisal Ibrahim

Arifah Fasha Rosmani

Nurzaid Muhd Zain

ISBN: 978-1-365-48255-7

FOREWORD

The publication of this book, CRINN (Computing Research and Innovation), Volume 1, November 2016, is a compilation of peer-reviewed research papers, technical and concept papers and innovations among the academicians from Faculty of Computer and Mathematical Sciences, Universiti Teknologi MARA, Perlis Branch, and other universities from all over Malaysia. This volume comprises of 14 scholarly articles from Computer Sciences, Mathematical Sciences, Computer Network and Data Communications and Information Technology and System Sciences fields.

Universities are now focusing on research as it has become central to both social and economic performance in its value for knowledge and innovation. Therefore, this volume, also serves as a sharing centre for every faculty members and others to share their research findings, experiences and innovations.

I would like to take this opportunity to thank and congratulate the authors for their contributions. My congratulations are also extended to the editors for putting together the contributions into a cohesive and readable form.

Assoc. Prof. Rohana Alias
Head
Faculty of Computer and Mathematical Sciences
Universiti Teknologi MARA
Perlis Branch
MALAYSIA

TABLE OF CONTENTS

SECTION I   COMPUTER & MATHEMATICAL SCIENCES

SECTION II   COMPUTER NETWORK & DATA COMMUNICATIONS

SECTION III **INFORMATION TECHNOLOGY & SYSTEM
SCIENCES**

Article	Title	Page

SECTION I:

COMPUTER
&
MATHEMATICAL
SCIENCES

Article 1

The Uncommon Approaches of Teaching the Programming Courses: The Perspective of Experienced Lecturers

Jamal Othman, Naemah Abdul Wahab
Department of Computer & Mathematical Sciences
Universiti Teknologi MARA Pulau Pinang Branch

Abstract

Programming courses have become one of the important courses for all sciences programs which are offered at the tertiary level (university). Currently, the students are compulsory to enroll in at least one basic programming course in order to fulfill the requirement of the university. The university needs more experienced lecturers to teach the programming courses. Most of the students are not interested in programming subject and they have considered the programming course as a high failure rate course. As a lecturer, we should be able to change their negative perception and motivate the students to use and apply the programming skills in their life.

Keywords: *teaching, experiences, approaches, programming, mentor & mentee, courseware*

Introduction

Teaching programming courses is not an easy task. In a paper by Abid (2011), he mentioned that Rist (1996) has acknowledged the lacking in professional and expert skills in programming language by novice learners as one of the main reasons of the program comprehension difficulties. It is a challenging task to make the students understand the topic that sometimes, the lecturers are required to use creative and innovative teaching methods in their class lessons. Only lecturers who taught the programming subjects will understand the complications and challenges faced in the process of teaching and learning of programming courses.

Most of the students who registered for these courses are considered as beginners with zero knowledge, and it is the responsibility of the course instructor to produce a valuable and knowledgeable human capital with an outstanding programming techniques. According to Gomes and Areiad (2008) the programming courses are generally labeled as difficult and the dropout rate is quite worried. Most of the students have set in their mind that the programming subject is a high failure rate course. They are overshadowed by this negative perception that they do not realize their hidden potential in programming skills.

In general, for those students who are specialized in computer science or any programming fields, they must enroll in at least 3 programming courses throughout their studies. The students should be able to grasp the concepts of programming techniques before they applied for industrial training or employment. Riley (1981) has identified the major problems of our students are the lack of skills in problem solving and analytical skills. The students should be exposed on the real problem and reduce the theoretical orientation of teaching approach. Most of the ICT industries have set the basic requirement for the graduates to have a good skill in programming methods.

This article will be discussing about the lecturers' perspectives and their teaching experiences on programming courses to two different categories of students, the beginner's groups and the intermediate as well as advanced students groups.

Teaching the beginners is a very exhausting process as the course instructors have to reiterate a simple topic repeatedly. Normally, you will need a longer period of time to cover a simple topic and in some worst cases; you have to recap the previous chapter after teaching the same topics for many weeks. Riley (1981) has identified the major problems of our students are the lack of skills in problem solving and analytical skills.

The students should be exposed on the real problem and reduce the theoretical orientation of teaching approach. This is one of the challenging parts and parcel of becoming a lecturer. Experiencing of failure rate more than 50% in a programming course is a common situation for all the lecturers. It is a very tough obligation when you are appointed by the Dean of Faculty to teach the programming course for the beginners. Moreover, if the basic academic qualification of the students' enrollment is very low, then it becomes a very excruciating experience to all programming lecturers throughout the entire semester.

In realizing the seriousness of these issues, several workshops and seminars have been conducted by the faculty and campuses to come out with the best solution to overcome this problem. Some of the solutions outlined are considered irrational because it has never been implemented but it is foreseen to be capable of producing a realistic outcome. Some solutions are impossible to be implemented because it will give additional tasks or workload to the lecturers. The best solution now is to come up with an easy, realistic, effective and practical way that does not require additional workload with acceptable approach to tackle the existing problem.

Methodology

There are many methods of effective teaching for programming courses. According to Zhou and Jin (2010), it is important to have good programming courses teaching quality as it will influence the learner's programming skills and computer application when they are working in the industry.

To begin with, lecturers **encourage the students to do a lot of exercises** by drilling through the pass year's examination questions and discussing the answers with their lecturer. By doing this, the learners not only concentrate on answering the questions but it also exposed the student to the precise method of writing the answer according to the answer scheme or lecturer's expectation. However, not all the lecturers including us, agreed to these common practices. This customary method in reality guided the students to become exam-oriented and narrowed up the scope of developing their programming abilities. It will only assist them in achieving good result in their final examination. Students know that some questions from the pass year's examination will be asked again in the upcoming examination, thus the scenarios of memorizing and targeting for certain questions or some particular topics also happened in our education system. Another reason, which contributed to the student's weakness in programming skill is due to the current education system that still depends on examination systems, nevertheless is very much lacking in hands-on programming practices exposures.

Maheshwari (1997) has expressed programming lessons should employ systematically designed direct instruction activities, rich in feedback and practice opportunities. Programming activities should be exposed with problem solving strategies such as planning, simplification and modeling. Teaching strategy should give high impact on students' knowledge and their ability to apply the knowledge.

Next, in the present education systems, **we should expose the students to a variety of assessments** such as assignments, quizzes, tests, project and final examination. In a study by Ramirez and Munoz (2014), they pointed out that assessment such as programming project enhances learner's programming comprehension as the students get the opportunity to apply their programming knowledge and abilities during the project development and implementation. From our past experiences, students tend to copy the assignment from their peers.

Furthermore, the assignment will not be an effective method of evaluation if you are giving the same question to each student. Therefore, we suggested the course instructors to give a new question to each of their students to be solved within 15 minutes during the practical programming laboratory session. This technique will determine whether the assignment presented to the lecturers is originally prepared by the student's or copied from another person. We have practiced this method for several semesters and we do not have to worry about their final examination because the students are capable of solving any types of question given to them. Additionally, they are also competent to present different kinds of unique answers or solutions and outstanding methods of problem-solving in answering the programming question.

Another method of teaching that we have implemented to our students are by **enquiring them to create questions, which are related to the current topic learned during the class lesson**. The lecturers are not required to answer the question; however, the questions will be answered by the remaining group of students. This method is normally applied in suggesting or proposing the topic for student's final year project. We should also apply this technique in programming courses to encourage students in becoming a creative thinker. By asking the students to create the questions, we are able to identify the level of students' knowledge in the programming topic, inspiring creativity in producing the questions, encourage ability to develop the question according to the degree of difficulties and finally, the course instructors are able to create a database of questions bank.

Nevertheless, you have to make sure that the students really understand the overall concepts of a topic before this practice can be implemented. We have tested this method for a couple of semesters and we found that the outcome is excellent. This teaching approach will really benefit both students and lecturers because it stimulates the elements of knowledge sharing if we are able to implement it successfully.

As a lecturer, we always **encourage the students to ask questions**. Nevertheless, do you think that this is really effective? From our observation, it only assists a small group of students. Flowerdew and Miller (1995) found that the Asian students are actually shy of asking questions to the lecturer. They are concerned if they asked the wrong or silly questions, asking for a personal reason, asked to be commended or the answer of the question can be obviously found in any textbooks. In contrast to the western students, they ask questions because they believe they have the rights to inquire.

Mentor and mentee systems, which is practiced for three semesters, seems effective in motivating the students to improve the programming skills and logical thinking, boost up confidence level and creating the programming interests. The mentor and mentee systems are handled by students themselves. The lecturers must ensure that the group of mentor and mentee system should include a person who is very proficient in programming language and skills. This person will act as a facilitator and mentor who are capable to create stimulating environment to all the mentees. In a study conducted at Monash University, Freeman, Jaeger and Brougham (2004) concluded that group work brought advantages for the students since working in group "can make computer coding more accessible to those with minimal or no background in this field". In turn, this may contribute to a higher level of programming aptitude and programmer confidence.

Another preferable method by **students is learning through examples**. The lecturers must show and explain many examples to students before they can understand the concepts of programming logics. Silva et al. (2003) had mentioned that the examples should be practical and interesting. Moreover, Zhou and Jin (2010) added that some universities provided programming examples resources on their websites for student's easy acquirement to improve the learner's interest, motivation, skills and decreasing their learning time. The examples should be from different perspectives, situations, conditions, cases or problems. The students are required to do a project will prefer the course instructors to show samples of their senior's project based on our experiences.

Thus, from there, they will get some ideas to produce the project proposal. From the lecturer's point of view, this practice is not considered as a plagiarism, but it is a way to provide the students with a basic overview and rough idea of a project proposal as well as the lecturer's expectation of the project requirements from their students. Moreover, as a lecturer, we will be very amazed and totally pleased to see that most of our students will be presenting an excellent completed task beyond our expectation that fulfill every requirement. Furthermore, we believe that through the implementation process of this project, it enhances their programming skills as well as improving their interpersonal and intrapersonal communication.

Other than that, the **lecturers should encourage the students to explore more examples from the websites**. According to Chapman (2002) the Internet is a relatively the most important channel to retrieve valuable resources and contains huge quantities of information. Nowadays, you will realize that the answers of the project given to the students are available in the websites. In fact, hundreds of project samples can be found on the Internet and are free to be downloaded. Therefore, the students will have a tendency to download the answer and modify the source code of a programming project according to the requirement of the questions. This norm amongst the students is difficult to be controlled. However, since the lecturer must make sure the originality of the project, their students should be allowed to reproduce the project but with a few conditions. They must understand the technicality of the source code, modify the source code or sample of the application according to the project or user's requirements and finally customize it according to lecturer's specifications or the company's operation.

The same situation happens in a working environment when the lecturers are required to do a research. Some studies particularly involving the research on project development, has been conducted by other academicians, thus, most of the source code can be downloaded from the open source websites. We are welcomed to download the source code without any violation to the copyright issues. Another channel to get the source code is by joining the open source community. This community will assist you in solving any technical problems or sharing specific source code that fulfills most of your requirements. Interestingly, we will receive a prompt reply or the sample source code within 3 days of our inquiry.

Another method of effective teaching of programming courses is by **providing the appropriate courseware for the students**. The courseware should be related to the topics covered in the syllabus. It should be interesting, but importantly, enable the students to understand the concepts, and at same time will attract the students' interest on programming courses. We have applied this technique to the programming courses and the outcome is positively unexpected. Some courseware has inserted elements of humor; with user-friendly designs that inspires the students to comprehend the programming topics easily. In addition, the lecturer's workload can be reduced since the courseware supports the students to learn each topic individually. To provide stimulating problems for students to solve, the environment needs to provide a rich set of graphical capabilities such as 3D features, as mentioned by Carlisle, et al. (2005). Soloways (1998) has mentioned in his article that the creativity of lecturer of applying animation to show program execution will minimize the students' difficulties.

The final teaching method that we are going to proposed will be it terms of the number of students in a group or classroom. **The size of the group should not exceed 25 students**. A bigger number of students in a group will result in fewer students focus on the topics that are taught and you as a lecturer cannot deliver the knowledge effectively. Programming requires more examples and exercises practiced by the students. Working with a small number of students allows a higher degree of interaction and discussion opportunities in the class. Brown and Atkins (1996) proposed this technique and it is applicable in technical subjects such as the programming paper. Studies on small groups have also been developed by social psychologists, Argyle (1983), who suggested that working with twenty students is the limit for developing good interaction.

Conclusion

In conclusion, the methodologies that have been mentioned in this article are based on the lecturers' experiences. We cannot presume that these methodologies are totally effective. Nevertheless, you can apply the methodology in your teaching and establish the effectiveness. There are many articles discussed on these matters and we have perceived that most of it is the subset of methods that have been mentioned in this article.

References

Abid, S.H., Zehra, S. and Iftikhar, H. (2011). *Using Computer Aided Language Software for Teaching and Self-learning*. In Proceeding: 14th International Conference on Interactive Collaborative Learning (ICL2011), pp. 102-106.

Argyle, M., *The Psychology of Interpersonal Behavior*, 4th ed: Penguin, London, 1983.

Brown, G. and Atkins, M., *Effective Teaching in Higher Education:Routledge*, 1996.

Carlisle, M. C., Wilson, T. A., Humphries, J. W., and Hadfield, S. M. 2005. *RAPTOR: a visual programming environment for teaching algorithmic problem solving*. In proceedings of the 36th SIGCSE Technical Symposium on Computer Science Education. ACM Press, 176-180.

Chapman, L. (2002). *Russian roulette or Pandora's box: use of Internet as a research tool*. Paper presented at VALA 2002. 11th Biennial Conference and Exhibition, 6-8 February, 2002, Melbourne. Victoria, Australia: Victorian Association for Library Automation Inc. Retrieved 24 December, 2006, from
http://www.vala.org.au/vala2002/2002pdf/18Chpmn.pdf

Flowerdew, J. & Miller, L. (1995). *On the notion of culture in L2 lectures*. TESOL Quarterly, 29(2)345-373.

Freeman, S. F., Jaeger, B. K. and Brougham, J. C., *Pair Programming: More Learning and Less Anxiety in a First Programming Course*, Vol. 2004, 2002.

Gomes, A., Areias, C. M., Henriques, J. & Mendes, A. (2008). *Aprendizagem de programação de computadores:dificuldades e ferramentas de suporte*. Revista Portuguesa De Pedagogia, 42, 2, 161–179.

Kessler, C. & Anderson, J. (1989). *Learning flow of control: recursive and iterative procedures*. In Soloway & Spohrer: Studying the Novice Programmer, pp. 229-260.

Maheshwari, P. (1997). *Improving the learning environment in first-year programming: Integrating lectures, tutorials, and laboratories*. Journal of Computers in Mathematics and Science Teaching, 16(1), 111-131.

Ramirez L., A., Munoz D., F. 2015. *Increasing practical lessons and inclusion of applied examples to motivate university students during programming courses*. In : Journal of the Social and Behavioral Sciences, Vol. 176, pp. 552-564.

Riley, D. (1981). Proceedings from Technical Symposium on Computer Science Education '81: Proceedings of the twelfth SIGCSE Technical Symposium on Computer Science Education, pp. 244-251, New York: ACM Press

Rist, R. (1996). *Teaching Eiffel as a first language.* In: Journal of Object-Oriented Programming, Vol. 9, pp. 30-41.

Silva, I.,H., Pacheco, O. and Tavares, J., *Effects of Curriculum Adjustments on First-Year Programming Courses: Students' Performance and achievement*, presented at 33rd ASEE/IEEE Frontiers in Education Conference, Boulder, Colorado, 2003, p. 3.

Soloway, E. M. (1986). *Learning to program = learning to construct mechanisms and explanations.* Communications of the ACM, 29, 850–858

Zhou Q., Jin J. 2010. *A Novel Student-Centered Teaching Reform on Programming Courses.* In proceedings of the International Conference on E-Health Networking, Digital Ecosystems and Technologies. IEEE, 221-223.

Article 2

3D Face Candidate Region Detection Using Background Subtraction

Zulfikri Paidi, Nurzaid Muhd Zain
Faculty of Computer & Mathematical Sciences
Universiti Teknologi MARA Perlis Branch

Abstract

In this paper, we have explored 3D face candidate region detection using background subtraction. Our focus is to solve the first challenge in face registration, which is to detect and identify face region. From the experiment, it shows some promising results related to using background subtraction in face candidate region detection algorithm. Firstly, we have succeeded in generating an oval shape for boundary region detection. Secondly, our face candidate region detection rate in percentage using background subtraction is 72.5% higher compared when background subtraction is excluded, which achieved only 60% of success rate.

Keywords: 3D face recognition; feature extraction, image registration

Introduction

Human face for detection and recognition is an active research area in computer vision. Three main stages in implementing automatic face recognition system are; (i) face registration, (ii) face feature extraction, and (iii) face matching. Face registration can be defined as a mapping process of two interest point's position at same point location from two different images of same scene taken at different times, from different viewpoints, and/or by different sensors (Brown, 1992; Zitová & Flusser, 2003; Crum, Hartkens & Hill, 2004; Wyawahare, Patil & Abhyankar, 2009; Boughorbel, Mercimek, Koschan & Abidi, 2010).

Face registration is the most important and crucial stage as to achieve good performance in face recognition. Three main challenges in face registration are; first is to detect and identify face region. Second is to extract facial feature points from the face region detected. Third is to establish correspondence of facial feature points extracted from the face region. In this paper, our focus is to solve the first challenge in face registration, which is to detect and identify face region. Our objective for face detection is to prepare face candidate region. In doing so, we proposed to use background subtraction on skin colour as our face detection method.

Previous Work

Research on detecting and identifying face region demands a lot of time and effort. This has been justified by (Li, 2005), which has listed much of the works in face detection by summarizing the problems as shown in Figure 1, and methods to resolve it as shown in Table 1.

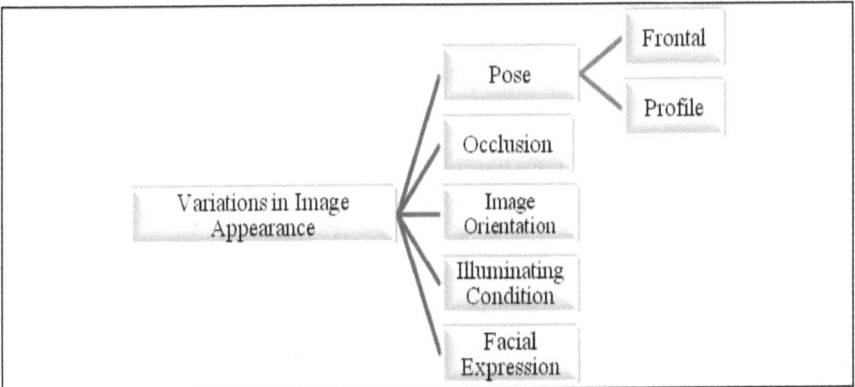

Figure 1: Problems in face detection caused from variations in image appearance (Li, 2005)

Table 1. Face Detection Methods

METHODS	PURPOSES
Template-matching methods	Used for face localization and detection by computing the correlation of an input image to a standard face pattern
Feature invariant approaches	Used for feature detection of eyes, mouth, ears, nose, etc
Appearance-based methods	Used for face detection with eigenface, neural network, and information theoretical approach

Other method that has been actively exercised in face detection is based on colour space detection. Several new approaches in face detection are lighting compensation (Hsu, Abdel-Mottaleb, &

Jain, 2002), colour distance map (Abdullah-Al-Wadud, Shoyaib, & Chae, 2008), adaptive skin colour segmentation algorithm based on Gaussian Mixture Model (Hassanpour, Shahbahrami, & Wong, 2008), and combination of skin colour detection with background subtraction(Li, Suhr, Kim, Jung, & Kim, 2010).

Methods
In this paper, we are proposing to use background subtraction on skin color for face detection. Based from previous face detection algorithm in (Hsu et al., 2002; Li et al., 2010; Wei & Lee, 2010), we propose to implement face candidate region detection algorithm as shown in Figure 2.

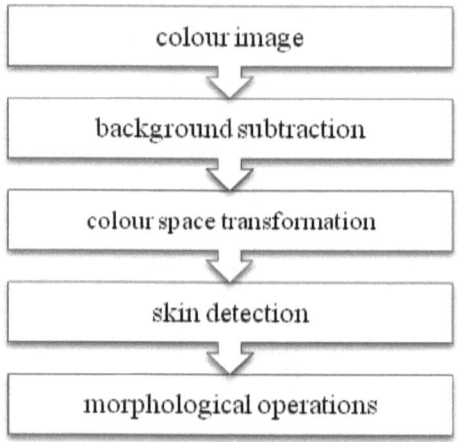

Figure 2: Face candidate region detection algorithm

Experiments
We performed portions of the research in this paper using the CASIA-3D FaceV1 collected by the Chinese Academy of Sciences' Institute of Automation (CASIA). In this experiment, we have select 10 individuals with eight models each. Most of the face models selected is frontal pose image. Facial expressions exist on each models are; neutral, smile, laugh, anger, surprise, and eye close. Illumination variation control is under office light. Figure 3 shows a sample of 3D face image from CASIA database.

Figure 3: CASIA 3D face image frontal view with neutral expression.

The 3D face image is taken from frontal views with some unnecessary regions such as shoulder, neck, and ears. Using face candidate region detection algorithm as in Figure 2, we run the experiment to obtain only the face candidate region. The first step in executing the algorithm is to read the colour image as input data. In second step, we extract the foreground and background image. The background image is subtracted from its colour image to produced image as in Figure 4.

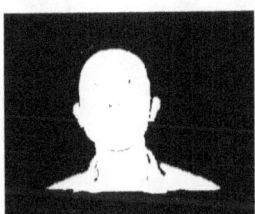

Figure 4: Background subtraction image

The third step in the algorithm is to transform the image colour space. We follow approaches by (Hsu et al., 2002) to execute this step. The result of the image is as shown in Figure 5.

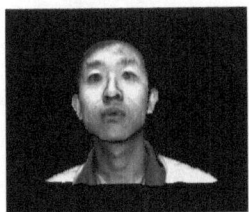

Figure 5: Lighting compensation

The fourth step is to detect the skin colour image. The image is shown in Figure 6.

Figure 6: Skin detection

The fifth step in the algorithm is to implement the morphological operations. In this step, we have executed three morphological operations in sequences as follows: fill holes, erosion and dilation. The image outputs from the operations are as shown in Figure 7.

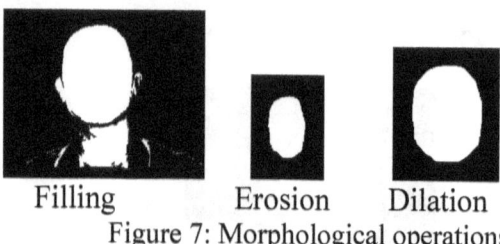

Filling   Erosion   Dilation

Figure 7: Morphological operations

The output for face candidate region detection is as Figure 8.

Figure 8: Face candidate region detection

Results

We have gathered output from the above experiments for image analysing. Before we start analysing the output, we have made some categorization on successful and unsuccessful face candidate region detection. Four categories have been identified and listed as in Table 2.

Table 2. Categorization for Successful and Unsuccessful Face Candidate Region Detection

CATEGORY	IMAGE
Successful region candidate detected	or
Successful with additional unwanted region/extension	or
At least one feature point component is detected	
Unsuccessful region candidate detected	
	Zero region is detected

We also have prepared another face candidate region detection experiment using the same algorithm, excluding the background subtraction step. This other set of experiments is prepared for comparison purposes. Some output examples from both experiments for comparison are shown as in Figure 9 and Figure 10.

Figure 9: Face candidate region detection without background subtraction

Figure 10: Face candidate region detection using background subtraction

We have analysed the image based on two factors; specifically in region boundary detection and percentage of a successful detection. Comparing the face candidate region detection output in Figure 9 and Figure 10, we found that face candidate region detection using background subtraction have captured the face boundary more specifically. The almost oval like or ellipse-like shape boundary created while using background subtraction have given advantages for next level feature point extraction processing. Compared to the algorithm that are not using background subtraction, we have found that most of the neck area is still been detected. This unnecessarily and unwanted region might give uncorrected result during extracting facial feature point stages.

For measuring the success rate on face candidate region detection, we have followed Table 2 rule on categorization for successful and unsuccessful face candidate region detection and combined it with results as in Figure 9 and Figure 10. Based on the finding, we can measure the success rate between both face candidate region detection using background subtraction and the excluded background subtraction as follows; the success rate for face candidate region detection using background subtraction is 72.5% and face candidate region detection without background subtraction is 60%.

Conclusion

In this paper, we have explored 3D face candidate region detection using background subtraction. Our focus is to solve the first challenge in face registration, which is about detecting and identifying face region. Results from the first challenge are then been used for the second challenge, which is to extract facial feature points from the face region detected.

Methodologically, we have designed an algorithm for background subtraction to be executed at the early steps of the algorithm. We have also created face candidate region detection without inserting background subtraction function. This other set of experiments is prepared for comparison purposes.

From image analysis, two factors on detecting specifics region boundary and percentage of a success rate have been identified. Based on those two factors, we found that face candidate region detection using background subtraction have given some promising results to be used for the next level of feature point extraction processing.

References

Abdullah-Al-Wadud, M., Shoyaib, M., & Chae, O. (2008). A Skin Detection Approach Based on Color Distance Map. *EURASIP Journal on Advances in Signal Processing, 2008*(1), 814283. https://doi.org/10.1155/2008/814283

Akinlar, M. A. (2009). A new Method for nonrigid Registration of 3D Images. *PhD Thesis*, (August).

Boughorbel, F., Mercimek, M., Koschan, A., & Abidi, M. (2010). A new method for the registration of three-dimensional point-sets: The Gaussian Fields framework. *Image and Vision Computing, 28*(1), 124–137. https://doi.org/10.1016/j.imavis.2009.05.003

Brown, L. G. (1992). A survey of image registration techniques. *ACM Computing Surveys, 24*(4), 325–376. https://doi.org/10.1145/146370.146374

Crum, W. R., Hartkens, T., & Hill, D. L. G. (2004). Non-rigid image registration: theory and practice. *The British Journal of Radiology, 77*(suppl_2), S140–S153. https://doi.org/10.1259/bjr/25329214

Hassanpour, R., Shahbahrami, A., & Wong, S. (2008). Adaptive Gaussian Mixture Model for Skin Color Segmentation. *World Academy of Science, Engineering and Technology, 31*(July), 1–6.

Hsu, R. L., Abdel-Mottaleb, M., & Jain, A. K. (2002). Face detection in color images. *IEEE Transactions on Pattern Analysis and Machine Intelligence, 24*(5), 696–706. https://doi.org/10.1109/34.1000242

Li, G., Suhr, J. K., Kim, D., Jung, H. G., & Kim, J. (2010). Minimizing false detection of skin color by using background subtraction. *International Conference on Electronics, Informations and Communications (ICEIC)*, 5–7.

Li, S. Z. (2005). Face Detection. *Learning, 3*(9), 1–6. https://doi.org/10.1007/0-387-27257-7_2

Wei, L., & Lee, E. (2010). 3D Face Recognition Using Face Feature Points Based on Parallel Stereo Vision. *International Journal of Digital Content Technology and Its Applications, 4*(1), 86–95. https://doi.org/10.4156/jdcta.vol4.issue1.9

Wyawahare, M. V, Patil, P. M., & Abhyankar, H. K. (2009). Image Registration Techniques : An overview. *International Journal of Signal Processing, Image Processing and Pattern Recognition, 2*(3), 11–28.

Zitová, B., & Flusser, J. (2003). Image registration methods: A survey. *Image and Vision Computing, 21*(11), 977–1000. https://doi.org/10.1016/S0262-8856(03)00137-9

CASIA-3D FaceV1, http://biometrics.idealtest.org/

Article 3

Automatic Preharvest Grading of Harumanis Fruits

Khairul Adilah bt Ahmad
Faculty of Computer & Mathematical Sciences
Universiti Teknologi MARA Kedah Branch

Sharifah Lailee Syed Abdullah
Faculty of Computer & Mathematical Sciences
UniversitiTeknologi MARA Perlis Branch

Abstract
Fruit size is one of the most important features for grading Harumanis fruits. However, harvesting the fruit at the correct size is problematic for fruits growers. The aim of this paper is to discuss the use of image processing technique to classify the grade of Harumanis fruits before harvesting. This research adopted a computer vision methodology, which include image acquisition, image pre-processing, image segmentation, feature extraction and classification. The statistical analysis which used linear regression model showed that the size has high relationship with the Harumanis' weights and grades. The results showed that it is possible to estimate the weight of fruits before harvesting using image processing technique thus enabling fruits grower to grade their products efficiently.

Keywords: Image processing, Feature Extraction, Size, Weight, Linear regression analysis, Harumanis Mango fruits

Introduction

The quality of Harumanis mangoes is determine by the shape and size of the fruits. Harumanis shapes and sizes influence the market value and therefore, are important features in grading of the fruits (Ercisli, Sayinci, Kara, Yildiz, & Ozturk, 2012). However, as practiced by Federal Agriculture Marketing Authority (FAMA), Harumanis fruits' quality is determine by their weights which is a post-harvest processing. For fruits growers, it is important to be able to assess the quality of fruits before harvesting, as this situation has considerable influence on high quality fruits (Jha, Chopra, & Kingsly, 2007). Therefore, it is a need to change from traditional post harvest grading to automatic preharvest grading using computer vision technique. This technique imitate the abilities of humans by electronically and automatically grading fruits and offer non-destructive methods and produce more consistent results than humans.

In recent years, computer visions are most widely used for fruits sorting and size grading. Past researches have shown the success of applying image processing technique for non destructive grading of fruits such as papaya (Riyadi, Mustafa, Hussain, & Hamzah, 2007), mangoes (Ab Razak, Mahmod, Mohd Nazari, Khairul Adilah & Tajul Rosli, 2012; Ganiron, 2014; Naik, Patel, & Pandey, 2015; Teoh & Syaifudin, 2007), apple (Hazbavi, 2014) and banana (Mustafa et al., 2008).

The aim of this paper is to discuss the use of the image processing technique to classify the grade of Harumanis fruits before harvesting based on their sizes.

Methodology
This section discusses the material and methods use to extracts information from fruits' images to estimate the quality of Harumanis. This research adopted a computer vision methodology that includes image acquisition, image pre-processing, image segmentation, feature extraction and classification (Du & Sun, 2004; Gunasekaran, 1996). The Harumanis fruit samples used for this study were obtained from the Perlis Agriculture Department's farm in Bukit Bintang, Perlis, Malaysia.

i. Image acquisition and Pre-processing
Image acquisition is a process where images are captured using digital camera. For this study the distance between the camera and the fruit were fixed at 30 cm. The images captured were saved in RGB colour format before they are converted into grayscale image.

ii. Image Segmentation
Next, image segmentation was carried out using EmaBm algorithm (Mahmod, Sharifah Lailee, Khairul Adilah, Mohd Nazari & Ab Razak, 2016). This algorithm isolated the fruit

images from the background. The result of this process is a single contour of the fruit image which provide a pixels value of "0" and "1" as shown in Figure 1. This values are used to extract the features of the fruit.

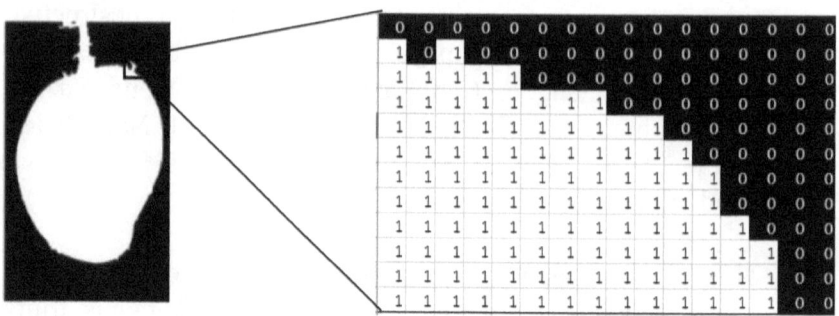

Figure 1: Pixel Value for Segmented Image

iii. Feature Extraction

For each fruit images, the features of the fruit were extracted by using image processing toolbox in the Matlab software. Area of the fruit was measured using total number of white pixels in the fruit contour region. The perimeter of fruit was measured as the total number of white pixels in the boundary contour region of binary image. The size estimation was used to determine the Harumanis grade. The size of Harumanis are graded as small, medium and large. The size of the fruits are measured using aspect ratio which are

$$Size = \frac{area}{perimeter}$$

iv. Size feature analysis

The size features was analyzed using SPSS. Variables which are area, perimeter and size were calculated and analyzed to determine the relationship between fruit weight and size. In regression analysis, a linear model was developed to estimate the weight of the Harumanis from size measurement. To evaluate the linear model, a 95% confidence and estimation intervals graph was used to verify that the linear model appropriately fit the data.

978-1-365-48255-7

Results and Discussion

Sample size measurements of three grade levels are shown in Table 1. Mean and standard deviation of the 105 training data set were 255.33g and 17.32 respectively.

Table 1: Contour Features for the Three Grades of Harumanis

Grade\nFeatures	Large\n(Grade A)	Medium\n(Grade B)	Small\n(Grade C)
Area	1159157	1080690	929711
Perimeter	4188.7274	4063.0878	3799.8401
Size	276.7325	265.9775	244.6711
Actual Weight (g)	373	342	299

For each relationship, a scatter plot was produced as shown in Figure 2, Figure 3 and Figure 4, then a regression analysis was performed. Each scatter plot was fitted with a least square regression line and the equation of the coefficient of determination (r^2). This equation is the estimation equation for weight value based on size.

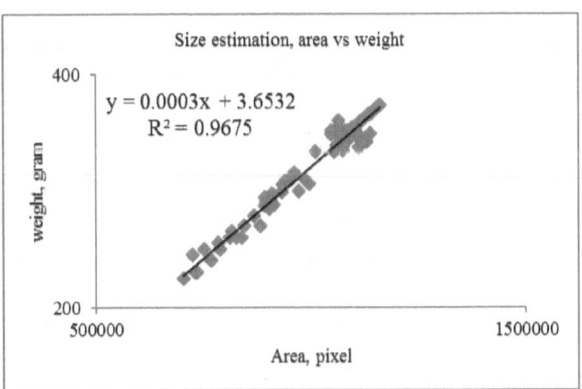

Figure 2: Scatter Plot for Area, A and Weight, W

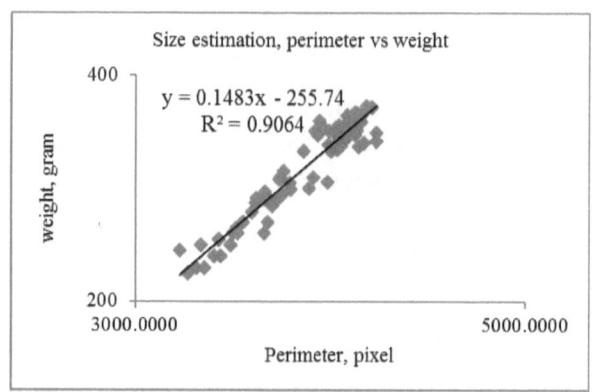

Figure 3: Scatter plot for Perimeter, P and Weight, W

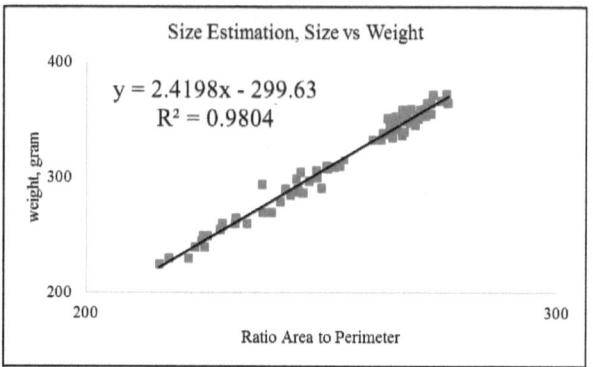

Figure 4: Scatter Plot forSize and Weight, W

A good estimation equation was selected based on R-squared (r^2) obtained for the correlation equation. Table 2 shows the estimation equations obtained for the contour area, perimeter, and size (in pixels) with their respective r^2.

Table 2: Weight Estimation Equations and their Respective r^2Values

Estimation Equations	r^2 values
Weight (gram) = 0.0003 x area + 3.6532	0.9675
Weight (gram) = 0.1483 x perimeter − 255.74	0.9064
Weight (gram) = 2.4198 x size + 184.33	0.9804

The results showed the varying correlation relationships for the features. This was seen in the high correlation coefficient values $r^2 = 0.9804$ obtained for the equations with weight used as the independent variable, in relation to the estimation equations with size measurement using aspect ratio. This indicates that the calculations of size measurement using aspect ratio area to perimeter performed a good mathematical descriptors to estimate weight from size measurements for determining the fruits grades.

The weight estimation from size measurements of Harumanis was computed using the ratio area to perimeter values via the feature extraction in the images analysis process. Statistical analysis of standard deviation was used for variability or diversity measurement. It shows how much variation there is from the mean. The lowest value of standard deviation of data indicates that the data points of size estimation are tend to be very close to the mean.

Root Mean Square Error (RMSE) represents the deviation between the actual weight and estimated weight from size measurements using image analysis. This parameter is used to compare two measurements from different level of errors. RMSE is frequently used to measure the differences between values predicted by a model and the values actually observed from the thing being modeled.

Table 3: Actual weight, Estimated Weight and Weight Different of Harumanis data set

Sample No	Actual Weight, gram	Estimation Weight, pixel	Weight Different
H1	373	370.01	2.9745
H2	351	346.44	5.5676
H3	356	361.99	0.0325
H4	354	349.48	1.5186
H5	355	355.87	(0.8696)
H6	353	343.66	(4.6738)
H7	367	367.15	(0.1217)
H8	365	360.01	4.9925
H9	372	362.91	9.0888
Mean			(0.0045)

Standard Deviation	5.9227
RMSE	5.8825
Min	(14.7988)
Max	19.2384

Table 3 shows nine sample Harumanis fruits with actual weights in gram, estimation weight in pixels and the weight difference between both values. The mean values of weight different between actual weights and estimation weight was 0.0045 grams. The standard deviation value of weight difference was 5.9227 grams. A low RMSE indicates high accuracy of the model. Results show that the size estimation gave the lowest values of RMSE at 5.8825. The weight estimated by the mathematical approximation was about 14.8 grams lower or 19.23 grams higher than the weight measured with digital scale. This means that the image analysis method based on the fruits' size measurements used in this experiment was sufficiently reliable to estimate the weights of the Harumanis mangoes before harvesting,

Conclusion

Measurements of the weight for Harumanis mangoes can be accomplished using EmaBm technique and size measurement. The present work has achieved the high-level in image processing and analysis technique to determine weight of Harumanis mangoes before harvesting.

References

Ab Razak, M., Mahmod, O., Mohd Nazari, A. B., Khairul Adilah, A., & Tajul Rosli, R. (2012). Mango size classification using RGB color sensor and fuzzy logic technique. *In Regional Conference on Science, Technology and Social Sciences*, pp. 287–296.

Du, C.-J., & Sun, D.-W. (2004). Shape extraction and classification of pizza base using computer vision. *Journal of Food Engineering*, 64(4), pp. 489–496.

Ercisli, S., Sayinci, B., Kara, M., Yildiz, C., & Ozturk, I. (2012). Determination of size and shape features of walnut (Juglans regia L.) cultivars using image processing. *Scientia Horticulturae*, 133, pp. 47–55.

Ganiron, T. J. (2014). Size Properties of Mangoes using Image Analysis. *International Journal of Bio-Science and Bio-Technology*, 6(2), pp. 31–42. http://doi.org/10.14257/ijbsbt.2014.6.2.03

Gunasekaran, S. (1996). Computer vision technology for food quality assurance, *71*(August).

Hazbavi, I. (2014). Shape and size grading of apple fruit (cv . Fuji) based on geometrical properties. *International Journal of Biosciences*, 4(12), pp.269–273.

Jha, S. N., Chopra, S., & Kingsly, a. R. P. (2007). Modeling of color values for nondestructive evaluation of maturity of mango. *Journal of Food Engineering*, 78(1), pp. 22–26.

Mahmod, O., Sharifah Lailee, S. A., Khairul Adilah, A., Mohd Nazari, A. B., & Ab Razak, M. (2016). The fusion of edge detection and mathematical morphology algorithm for shape boundary recognition. *Journal of Information and Communication Technology (JICT)*, 15(1), pp. 133–144.

Mustafa, N. B. A., Fuad, N. A., Ahmed, S. K., Abidin, A. A. Z., Ali, Z., Yit, W. B., & Sharrif, Z. A. M. (2008). Image Processing of an Agriculture Produce : Determination of Size and Ripeness of a Banana. *In ITSim 2008. International Symposium in Information Technology* (Vol. 1, pp. 1–7). IEEE. Retrieved from http://ieeexplore.ieee.org/

Naik, S., Patel, B., & Pandey, R. (2015). Shape, size and maturity features extraction with fuzzy classifier for non-destructive mango (Mangifera Indica L., cv . Kesar) grading. *In IEEE International Conference on Technological Innovations in ICT for Agriculture and Rural Development*, pp. 1–7.

Riyadi, S., Mustafa, M. M., Hussain, A., & Hamzah, A. (2007). Papaya fruit grading based on size using image analysis, pp. 645–648.

Teoh, C. C., & Syaifudin, A. R. M. (2007). Image processing and analysis techniques for estimating weight of Chokanan mangoes. *Journal of Tropical Agriculture and Food Science*, 35(1), pp.1 83–190.

Article 4

Travelling Choices Made Easier using Dijkstra Algorithm

Wardah Mohd Nor, Noraini Noordin
Faculty of Computer & Mathematical Sciences
Universiti Teknologi MARA Perlis Branch

Abstract

Current inflating high cost of living may affect mobility of students to commute between their university and any other destination. In an attempt to help solve or minimise the problem, several proposed travel alternative modes from this research may help students to identify the shortest path and minimum cost path in a journey. In finding the minimum total travel cost and shortest total completion time for a journey between two destinations, the step-by-step Dijkstra algorithm was applied in the time-dependent shortest path problem (TDSPP) and cost-dependent shortest path problem (CDSPP) in this research. Interestingly, both problems treated separately mapped out two different paths with two different costs. The former mapped out a route from UiTM Perlis Branch to Arau by taxi, train from Arau to Alor Setar, and Malaysia Airlines flights from Alor Setar to Kuala Lumpur and on to Johor Bahru. The other route was best described by taxi from Arau to Alor Setar, Air Asia flight from Alor Setar to Kuala Lumpur and train from Kuala Lumpur to Johor Bahru.

Keywords: *shortest path problem, dijkstra algorithm, network model, time-dependent SPP, cost-dependent SPP.*

Introduction

Economy of a country is very much affected by movement of goods and services through land, air and water (Nagurney, 2007). It is particularly important for students to move between two destinations. By constructing a network model to represent the journey between two destinations that involves multiple types of transportation, this study has been able to determine the shortest cost-efficient path between two destinations, in terms of time and money using Dijkstra algorithm In particular, this simple and well-known effective algorithm has been chosen to solve the time-dependent shortest path problem (TDSPP) and cost-dependent shortest path problem (CDSPP) in this research.

Literature Review

The models for both TDSPP and CDSPP were drawn separately.

i. Network Diagram

A network diagram consists of a set of nodes that are linked by arrows. It defines the relationship between nodes and edges, direction of edges, as well as cost of nodes and edges. It is denoted by (N, A), where N is a set of nodes and A is the set of edges (Taha, 2006). It is also an important mathematical program that has been applied in many fields like communication networks, social networks and scientific collaboration networks (Lloyd &Valeika, 2012). In addition, a network model can help to solve optimization problems such as transportation problem, critical path, shortest path, minimum cost flow problems, and many more. In this study, a network model has been used to determine the shortest path from UiTM Perlis Branch (UP) to Johor Bahru (JB) with minimum time and fare.

ii. The Shortest Path Problem (SPP)

According to Kamiński et al. (2011), SPP finds the path between two nodes in a graph that minimizes the sum of the weights of its constituent edges. For the current research, SPP has helped to find the best combination of transportation modes that would give shortest time and minimum cost between each pair of nodes. d_{ij}, travel time needed from node i to node j, $(i, j) \in A$ has been used to represent delay time. Delay time is time-dependent on the start time for the travel. In other words, the function $d_{ij}(t)$ returns time to travel from i to j when leaving i at time t, thus arrival time at node j is $t+d_{ij}(t)$ (Kamiński et al., 2011). With respect to the current research, the delay function has been defined for deterministic discrete time problems, where the time on each arc was known and finite with certainty.

iii. Dijkstra Algorithm

Dijkstra algorithm is especially effective to solve a single-source shortest path problem in a directed graph with nonnegative weight. It is considered to be a simpler but faster version of Ford's algorithm. However, weight functions needed to be identified ahead of time, are monotonic and do not change (Abbasi & Ebrahimnejad, 2011).

Dijkstra maintains an array of provisional distance, d for each node and size of the search space is $O(n^2)$ and $n/2$ nodes on the average. When all target nodes are reached, the path can be stopped (Murota & Shioura, 2014).

In this algorithm, set D for all extended nodes and set U for unintended nodes are fixed, set D will increase as the minimal weight node from U is updated and the procedures will continue until all nodes are in D (Jasika et al., 2012). Figure 1 displays the step-by-step application of this algorithm as adapted from Jasika et al. (2012) and is explained below:

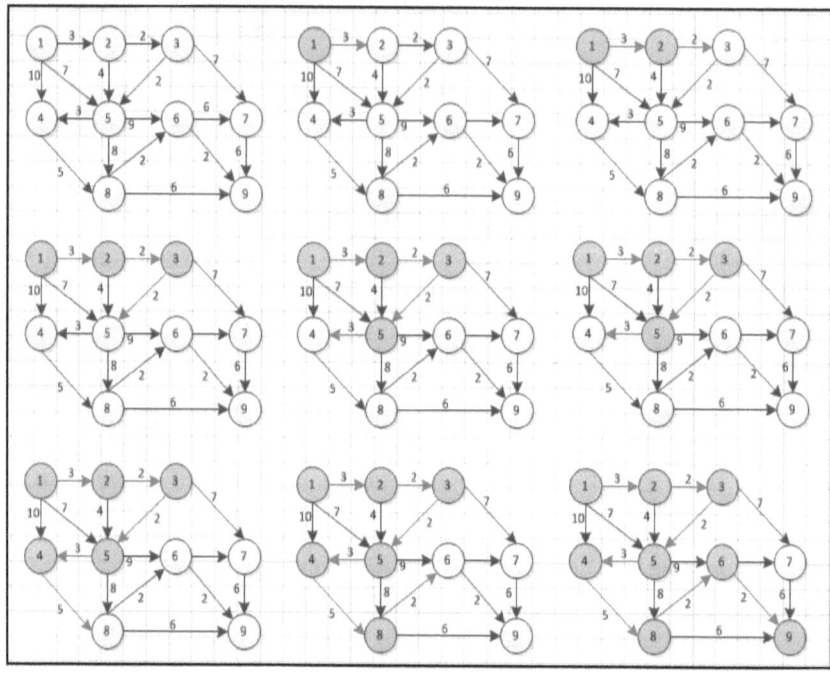

Figure 1: Dijkstra algorithm in steps

1. Assign zero weighted value to a source node, s which is tagged as permanent, (0, p). This now becomes the current node. Every other node is assigned a distance value of ∞ and is tagged as temporary (∞, t).

2. Letting i be the index of the current node, find another temporary tagged node that can be connected with i and

update the distance values of (i,j) as $newd_j = \min(d_j, d_i + c_{ij})$, c_{ij} is the cost of the link (i,j).

3. Determine a node j with the smallest distance value d_j among all nodes connected with i, such that, $\min_j d_j = d_j^*$.

4. Change the label of node j^* to permanent and designate it as the current node.

5. By repeating all steps beginning step 2, the path has reached the end when all nodes have been permanently tagged.

Methodology

An analysis of the journey from UP to JB was done. It involved three common types of transport: bus, train, and airplanes. Selected transportation agencies were Transnasional, Sri Maju, City Express, AirAsia, Malaysia Airlines (MAS), Malindo Air, and Keretapi Tanah Melayu (KTM) Berhad.

i. Current Alternatives for Travel Routes out of UP

Firstly, to apply the Dijkstra algorithm, the assumptions made were i) UP was the start point, ii) JB was the terminal point, iii) varying price of flight tickets, and iv) mode of transport to the first activity port was taxi. Secondly, 245 selection of travel paths in the three-phase journey from UP to JB were constructed based on the condition that taxi was the mode of travels beginning from A (UP - Arau), C (UP - Alor Setar), and D (UP - Kangar).

ii. Network Model Construction

The first step in finding the shortest path is to determine activities that are related to the project (Marasovic and Marasovic, 2006), the first step to find the shortest path in a journey is to list the activities involved. Based on 21 activities, a precedence table as shown in Table 1 was drawn.

Table 1: Precedence Table

Task	Precedence	Description	Task	Precedence	Description
A	-	UP - Arau by taxi	S	A,B,C,D,E, F,G,H,I	Alor Setar - KL by MAS
B	A	Arau - Alor Setar by KTM	T	S	Dummies

C	-	UP - Alor Star by taxi	U	A,B,C,D,E,F,G,H,I	Alor Setar - KL by Malindo Air
D	-	UP - Kangar by taxi	V	U	Dummies
E	D	Kangar - Alor Setar by Sri Maju	W	J,K,L,M,N,O,P,Q,R,S,T,U,V	KL - JB by Sri Maju
F	D	Kangar – Alor Setar by Transnasional	X	W	Dummies
G	F	Dummies	Y	J,K,L,M,N,O,P,Q,R,S,T,U,V	KL - JB by Transnasional
H	D	Kangar – Alor Setar by City Express	Z	Y	Dummies
I	H	Dummies	AA	J,K,L,M,N,O,P,Q,R,S,T,U,V	KL - JB by City Express
J	A,B,C,D,E,F,G,H,I	Alor Setar - KL by Sri Maju	AB	AA	Dummies
K	J	Dummies	AC	J,K,L,M,N,O,P,Q,R,S,T,U,V	KL - JB by KTM
L	A,B,C,D,E,F,G,H,I	Alor Setar - KL by Transnasional	AD	J,K,L,M,N,O,P,Q,R,S,T,U,V	KL - JB by Air Asia
M	L	Dummies	AE	AD	Dummies
N	A,B,C,D,E,F,G,H,I	Alor Setar - KL by City Express	AF	J,K,L,M,N,O,P,Q,R,S,T,U,V	KL - JB by MAS
O	N	Dummies	AG	AG	Dummies
P	A,B,C,D,E,F,G,H,I	Alor Setar - KL by KTM	AH	J,K,L,M,N,O,P,Q,R,S,T,U,V	KL - JB by Malindo Air
Q	A,B,C,D,E,F,G,H,I	Alor Setar - KL by Air Asia	AI	AH	Dummies
R	Q	Dummies			

The activity-on-arc techniques were used to construct two models for the time-dependent shortest path problem (TDSPP) and cost-dependent shortest path problem (CDSPP). The network for CDSPP is shown in Figure 2. The weights were given in terms of money in the TDSPP network.

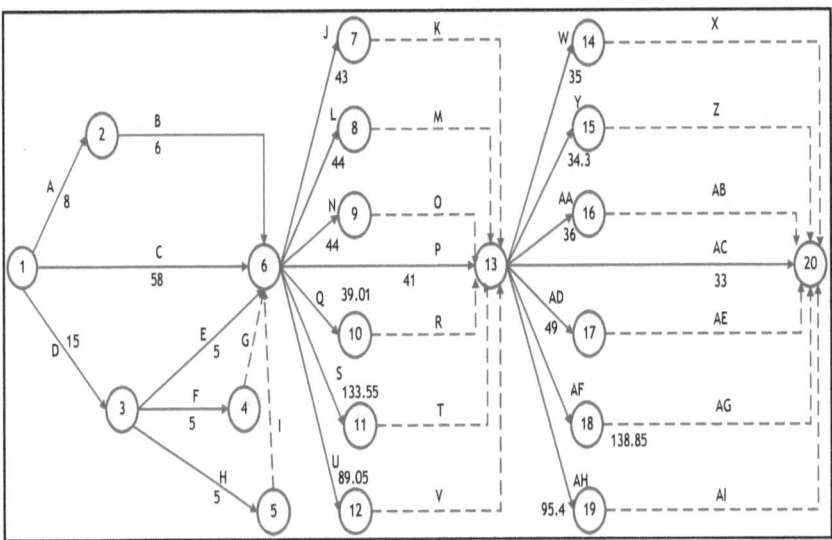

Figure 2: Cost-dependent shortest path problem network diagram

iii. Objective Function

By letting z to be the total time for a travel, eqn. 1 to 12 minimize time for each travel as follows:

$$\min z = \sum_{i=1}^{m}\sum_{j=1}^{m} d_{ij}x_{ij} + \sum_{i=m+1}^{n}\sum_{j=m+1}^{n} d_{ij}x_{ij} + \sum_{i=m+n+1}^{p}\sum_{j=m+n+1}^{p} d_{ij}x_{ij} \tag{1}$$

where,

m, n, p	=	total number of nodes at each stage respectively
i	=	start point
j	=	end point
d_{ij}	=	time travel from city i to city j

subject to:

978-1-365-48255-7

For nodes 1 to 6,

$$x_{ij} = \begin{cases} 1, & \text{if } x_{12}, x_{13}, \text{ or } x_{16} \text{ is selected} \\ 0, & \text{otherwise} \end{cases} \tag{2}$$

For nodes 2 to 6,

$$x_{ij} = \begin{cases} 1, & \text{if } x_{26} \text{ is selected} \\ 0, & \text{otherwise} \end{cases} \tag{3}$$

For nodes 3 to 6,

$$x_{ij} = \begin{cases} 1, & \text{if } x_{34}, x_{35}, \text{ or } x_{36} \text{ is selected} \\ 0, & \text{otherwise} \end{cases} \tag{4}$$

For nodes 6 to 13,

$$x_{ij} = \begin{cases} 1, & \text{if } x_{67}, x_{68}, x_{69}, x_{610}, x_{611}, x_{612}, \text{ or } x_{613} \text{ is selected} \\ 0, & \text{otherwise} \end{cases} \tag{5}$$

where, x_{713}, x_{813}, x_{913}, x_{1013}, x_{1113}, or x_{1213} are dummies

For nodes 13 to 20,

$$x_{ij} = \begin{cases} 1, & \text{if } x_{1314}, x_{1315}, x_{1316}, x_{1317}, x_{1318}, x_{1319}, \text{ or } x_{1320} \text{ is selected} \\ 0, & \text{otherwise} \end{cases} \tag{6}$$

where, x_{1420}, x_{1520}, x_{1620}, x_{1720}, x_{1820}, or x_{1920} are dummies

To calculate the shortest fare for this travel, the objective function (1) is adjusted with y as the minimum total time for a travel and f_{ij} as time travel from city i to city j.

Results and Discussions

Separate calculations were made for TDSPP and CDSPP. As shown in Figure 3, the shortest path for the CDSPP model was marked with red line by starting with node 1, UP. Similar procedures were carried out for TDSPP.

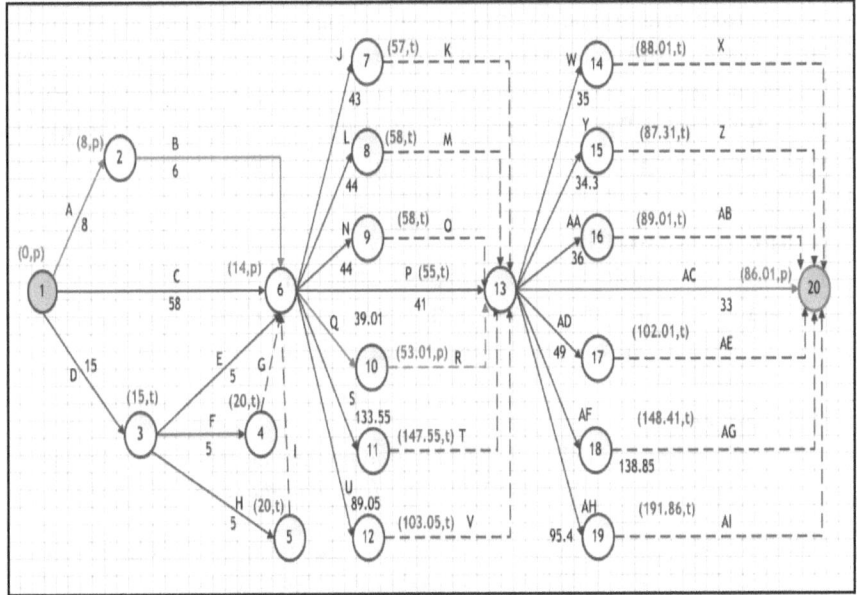

Figure 3: Result in step-by-step Dijkstra algorithm for CDSPP network model

In this research, the shortest path with a total cost of RM86.01 was described by UP – Arau by taxi, Arau – Alor Setar by taxi, Alor Setar – KL by AirAsia, and KL – JB by train. In contrast, the shortest path for TDSPP was identified by the path from UP – Arau by taxi, Arau – Alor Setar by train, Alor Setar – KL by Malaysia Airlines, and KL – JB by Malaysia Airlines. Total time calculated was 160 minutes or 2 hours and 40 minutes.

Conclusion

Due to time constraints on the duration of this study, TDSPP and CDSPP through a fixed sequence of nodes were treated separately. Using step-by-step Dijkstra algorithm, the minimum cost of RM86.01 was achieved in a longer time whereas the cost associated with TDSPP was RM286.40. These findings suggest that travellers have the option of choosing either a time-effective shortest path or cost-effective shortest path. The results from the step-by-step Dijkstra algorithm proved to be similar to results run in C programming. With additional transportations other than the three used in this research, the results would be more interesting.

In addition, the scope of this research may be widened to include areas other than transportation problems. Furthermore, the findings would also be interesting if the research were converted to a dynamic SPP by adding float time, or finding one shortest path for both time and cost by adding both SPP.

Acknowledgements

The authors would like to express our gratitude to Transnasional, Sri Maju, City Express, AirAsia, Malaysia Airlines, Malindo Air, and KTMB for allowing access to their data.

References

Abbasi, S., & Ebrahimnejad, S. (2011). Finding the Shortest Path in Dynamic Network using Labeling Algorithm. *International Journal of Business and Social Science, 2*(20).

Jasika, N., Alispahic, N., Elma, A., Ilvana, K., Elma, L., & Nosovic, N. (2012, 21-25 May 2012). *Dijkstra's shortest path algorithm serial and parallel execution performance analysis.* Paper presented at the MIPRO, 2012 Proceedings of the 35th International Convention.

Kamiński, M., Medvedev, P., & Milanič, M. (2011). Shortest paths between shortest paths. *Theoretical Computer Science, 412*(39), 5205-5210. doi: http://dx.doi.org/10.1016/j.tcs.2011.05.021

Lloyd, A. L., & Valeika, S. (2012). Network models in epidemiology: an overview *Complex Population Dynamics* (pp. 189-214): WORLD SCIENTIFIC.

Marasovic, J., & Marasovic, T. (2006, Sept. 29 2006-Oct. 1 2006). *CPM/PERT Project Planning Methods as E-Learning Optional Support.* Paper presented at the Software in Telecommunications and Computer Networks, 2006. SoftCOM 2006. International Conference on.

Murota, K., & Shioura, A. (2014). Dijkstra's algorithm and L-concave function maximization. *Mathematical Programming, 145*(1-2), 163-177. doi: http://dx.doi.org/10.1007/s10107-013-0643-2

Nagurney, A. (2007). Mathematical Models of Transportation and Networks.

Taha, H. A. (2006). *Operations Research: An Introduction (8th Edition)*: Prentice-Hall, Inc.

SECTION II:

COMPUTER NETWORK
&
DATA COMMUNICATIONS

Article 5

Raspyair: Self-Monitoring System for Wireless Intrusion Detection using Raspberry Pi

Mohd Nizam Osman, Mohd Syafiq Aiman Mohamad Zulrahim
Faculty of Computer & Mathematical Sciences
Universiti Teknologi MARA Perlis Branch

Mushahadah Maghribi
Department of Information Technology and Communication, PTSS Perlis

Abstract

This paper described a self-monitoring for wireless intrusion-detection system (IDS) using Raspberry Pi to enhance the security performance for personal computers. Nowadays, most of the personal computers are interconnected without wire. Therefore, everybody can easily connect to the Internet and indirectly exposed to the security issues, especially the safety of the confidential data. Sometimes, we do not know that someone is sniffing our network, even we do not realize that there was an intruder in our network due to most of the personal computers does not have the intruder monitoring system. To overcome this problem, we proposed a system for wireless monitoring and intruder detection for personal computer known as RaspyAir. This system was implemented using misuse detection approach, which is hybridization of tShark and Airodump-ng to capture the possibility of the traffic in the wireless environment. The brute-force algorithm is used to filterthe traffic using signature based detection technique. Then, RaspyAir was integrated with a credit card size single board computer, which is Raspberry Pi as an external tool for monitoring system. The developed system is then tested using code auditing and penetration testing to identify the achievement of the system. After applying the testing from Wireless Security Assessment Methodology (WSAM), a standard measure score is calculated to evaluate the degree of the security for the system. Hence, the result has shown the RaspyAir followed the security guidelines, fully secured, can be deployed for personal computer and significantly increase the security performance for monitoring wireless intrusion-detection system. Additionally, from the experiment conducted has confirmed that by using Raspberry Pi as an external tool, it consumed nine times less electrical power compared to the personal computer.

Keywords: Wireless, intrusion detection system (IDS), monitoring system, wireless security assessment methodology (WSAM), Raspberry Pi.

Introduction

In recent years, wireless networking has been experiencing an explosive growth, which resembles the rapid growth of the

Internet itself in the mid-1990s. According to the report by International Telecommunication Union (ITU), almost 40 percent of the world population has an internet connection (ICT Data and Statistics Division, 2015). Furthermore, wireless networking is the easiest way to set up an internet network. There are no obtrusive cables, and people are free to use their devices virtually anywhere in the coverage area. In addition, new devices can be added to the network just in minutes.

Nowadays, the wireless network becomes a necessity. In essence, a wireless network lets multiple devices in the coverage area, share the same broadband Internet connection, as well as talk to one another. The most common type of Internet network in today's home/work is a wireless network or also known Wi-Fi. At present, the range of Wi-Fi network is about 30-40 metres indoor and up to 100 metres outdoors. Besides, a high-powered Wi-Fi standard known as 802.11y is intended to boost outdoor up to 5000 metres, enabling for increased wireless operation for more users at much higher power than via traditional Wi-Fi equipment.

Connecting network to the internet access provides access to the huge amount of information. It allows people to share information across the globe. However, common nature of the Internet, which creates so many benefits, also offers the malicious users to access giant amount of targets. For this reason, an unsecured wireless network gives hackers the perfect gateway to access to a personal computer or an organization's internal network. Besides letting the hacker steal or destroy information on the network and giving him or her free Internet access, then the wireless network might also help him or her to carry out cyber-attack. Hence, this situation will make internet users vulnerable to data security risks. Indeed, since there is no way to identify a hacker on a network from the personal computers, which installed the wireless network, might be opened to the attack. Therefore, the users have responsibility to ensure the safety of the network from the intruder, especially on the security issues. This issue should be resolved by identifying the main causes, which most of the problems relate with the users who using the wireless network. Besides, the number of users using the wireless network tremendously increasing, then each user must have a monitoring system for wireless intrusion detection, which can be installed on the personal computer to monitor every activity occurs on the network.

Network monitoring activity refers to the ability of the system to notify the network administrator if there are failed in devices, and outage occurred in the network by monitoring the device to see the network traffic and log the information of network traffic (Zargar, Joshi, & Tipper, 2014). This is crucial for the network in order to analyse the performance and security of the network system. To observe the performance of the network, the performance metric are being used. For instances, throughput, average latency, bandwidth consumed, average delay, and mean batch service time. Meanwhile, network security is important to ensure the availability, confidentiality and integrity of the data transmission. There is a research conducted to study about network security of wireless home network and the result shown there were a lot of foreign IP addresses found in the traffic (Aspernäs & Simonsson, 2015). Therefore, it was confirmed that unauthorized users who are currently connected to the access point without us realizing it. Hence, the network performance will decrease because of massive traffic by unauthorized users.

On the other hand, the intrusion detection is the mechanism to detect any unusual network traffic and notify the user to take action. The unusual network traffic usually caused by the malicious user who sending out illegal packet to the network for any purposes. Hence, it will increase the respond of user to take action and prevent the threat from reaching the network resources. To overcome the problems, there must be some computer algorithms to analyse the pattern of the network traffic. There are varieties of approaches(Dmitry & Dennis, 2008; Jia & Chen, 2009; Makanju, Zincir-Heywood, & Milios, 2008) in the intrusion-detection system (IDS), which are behavioural, signature and combination of both. For instance, misuse detection use signature analysis of the network traffic by defined the lawless action and compare it with the observed object or based known system bug and intrusion pattern (Jia & Chen, 2009). Other researchers use collaborative intrusion, which combines many detection approaches (Mingqiang, Hui, & Qian, 2012). The advantages when using the collaborative intrusion-detection system, repairs some drawback of traditional cluster algorithm and achieving satisfaction performance. Unfortunately, the complexity of the algorithm caused of memory requirement and growth in the record number. On the other hand, collaborative IDS also cooperate with mobile agent and applying them into the intrusion-detection system, which an autonomous agent can provide the suitable, systematic and strong programming paradigm for shared application (Mo, Ma, & Xu, 2008). This approach reduces central processing unit (CPU) and memory usage.

There are varieties of techniques used in order to monitor the wireless intrusion detection. For instance, intrinsic monitoring which relies on IP extension headers in combination with formal behaviour models to gather information along the path in order to delegate monitoring functionality to the network devices (Höfig & Coşkun, 2009). Besides, G. Song (2012) uses two structures of the monitoring system, which are data display module and traffic monitoring module and make the monitoring system can monitor traffic in more than one computer, reduce the workload of network management and improve network traffic monitoring (Song, 2012).

As the technology becomes sophisticated, the wired connection moves to wireless connection and this technology widely used around the world. However, there were a lot of flaws associated with the wireless protocol that will attract the cyber-criminal to penetrate the network. For instances, it is possible for the malicious users to eavesdropping the communication in the wireless network and abuse the information. Hence, it is essential to have a system that can monitor for the wireless intrusion detection for all users. Moreover, the intrusion-detection system that existed today was integrated with the large scale of hardware.

Therefore, a save cost device is needed, and it can easily attach to the wireless network without any specific space configuration. Hence, we developed a self-monitoring system for wireless intrusion detection using Raspberry Pi as an external tool to enhance the security performance of the wireless network. Raspberry Pi is a single board computer, and it also can make any computational process for many applications (Agrawal & Singhal, 2015; Paramanathan et al., 2014; Soetedjo, Ashari, Mahmudi, & Nakhoda, 2014). There is a research conducted using Raspberry Pi as the intrusion-detection system with some limitations such as suffering lower network throughput(Aspernäs & Simonsson, 2015). The advantage of Raspberry Pi, it can operate same as computer but in small version and more interactive besides consumed less electricity.

Methodology
The study starts by studying previous research, journal, book and website that use intrusion-detection system (IDS) and monitoring system for wireless environment. From this study, a set of the guideline was produced to develop the monitoring system for wireless intrusion detection using Raspberry Pi (RaspyAir). This guideline mainly concerns with the intrusion-detection system, monitoring system, wireless technology and Raspberry Pi.

While developing the prototype, the RaspyAir used misuse detection approach. This approach was implemented signature based detection technique, which means that they operate by searching for a known identity or signature for each specific intrusion event. For that, all the network traffic will be filtered using brute-force algorithm and gave an alert to the user if an intruder detected. The network traffic is captured by using TShark and Airodump-ng. Besides, the RaspyAir was designed with two types of network analysis, which are real-time analysis and offline analysis. The real-time analysis is an analysis based on the current state of the wireless network, whereas the offline analysis is an analysis based on input of wireless traffic files type such as *.pcap* and *.cap*. Then, the RaspyAir will generate a report to the user, and user can simply print the report for future use.

After the development phase,the RaspyAir will be tested to identify the achievement of the security performance. This study conducts the penetration of testing, where the specific attacks will be launched to the system. The security testing of the system was done using Wireless Security Assessment Methodology (WSAM) by Karthik (2015). This is to ensure that the RaspyAir can provide a secure application.

WSAM provides a guideline for setting up a security standard, checking compliance, gathering firmware version for all types of devices, finding unapproved access point, checking if decoded movement is navigating the remote system and guaranteeing that feeble types of WEP (Wired Equivalent Privacy) are not being used. The assessment was made based on five types of attack, which are availability, access control, confidentiality, integrity and authentication attack (Karthik, 2015).

To have a standard measurement, score values for the attacks are defined in Table 1.

Table 1: Score value for the attack evaluation

Score Value	Scoring Meaning
1	Not Secure
2	Partly Secure
3	Fully Secure

At the end of testing, all scores will be summed up and the percentage will be calculated. This percentage will be analysed to determine whether the RaspyAir is secure or not. Table 2 represents the meaning of percentage in order to get the result or conclusion of the research for the RaspyAir.

Table 2: The definition of the security percentage calculated

Percentage	Definition
Less than 25%	The system failed to meet the guideline requirement for the types of attack.

26% - 50%	The system meets some of the guideline and helps eliminate some vulnerability but still need a lot of improvement.
51% - 79%	The system meets most of the guideline and is adequate to build a wireless security system.
80% - 100%	The system meets the guideline requirement and helps to build a good wireless security system.

Then, the overall percentage was calculated to classify whether the RaspyAir follows the security guideline or not and to determine whether the system developed can be deployed or not. Table 3 shows the meaning of the overall percentage towards the acceptance of the proposed system.

Table 3: The definition of the overall security percentage calculated

Percentage	Definition
Less than 50%	The system cannot be used and need a lot of improvements.
51% - 75%	The system can be used but partly secured and must be monitor by the developer.
76% - 100%	The system followed the security guidelines and fully secured. Therefore, it can be deployed.

Finally, the electricity consumption testing has been conducted to compare the electricity consumption between Raspberry Pi and HP Compaq Notebook. In order to measure the electricity consumption of the two computers, a Multifunctional Mini Ammeter was used.

Security Evaluation
The five different types of attack as suggested by the WSAM guideline were evaluated. The first attack is access control attack, which focuses on penetrating the wireless by evading the wireless security measure such as MAC filter and Wi-Fi port security to obtain unauthorized access. The second attack is wireless integrity attack which the attacker sends modified control, data and management frame over the wireless network to misdirect the wireless devices in order to perform denial-of-

service(DoS) attack. The third attack is confidentiality attack focuses on interception over the wireless network either in clear plain text or encrypted by Wi-Fi protocol. The fourth attack is availability attack prevents the legitimate user from accessing the access point via access point(AP)theft, beacon flood, authentication flood, temporal key integrity(TKIP) message integrity code(MIC) exploitation, de-authenticate flood, routing attacks Address Resolution Protocol(ARP) cache positioning and power saving attacks. Finally, we evaluate on authentication attack which the purpose is to steal identity information of Wi-Fi clients and to gain unauthorized access of the wireless network resources which can be happened over a course of time through application login theft, preshared key(PSK) cracking, shared key guessing, domain login cracking, identity theft, virtual private network(VPN) login cracking, lightweight extensible authentication protocol (LEAP) cracking and password speculation.

Research Results

To evaluate the security degree of RaspyAir, the study has successfully done fifteen attacks in the area of access control attack, wireless integrity attack, confidentiality attack, availability attack and authentication attacks on the home/work wireless network. Basically, the work involved finding the security bugs in order to evaluate the system. The score value was given for every type of attacks launched. Table 4 shows the score value.

Table 4: Wireless Security Evaluation Result

No.	Attacks	Score (1 - 3)
Access Control Attack		
1	Rough access point	3
2	Probing by wireless devices	3
3	Evil twin	3
	Total	**9/9**
Wireless Integrity Attack		
4	ARP request replay	2
5	WPA Bruteforce	3

6	KorekChopChop	3
7	Fragmentation	1
	Total	**9/12**
	Confidentiality Attack	
8	WEP key cracking	2
9	WPA migration mode attack	3
	Total	**5/6**
	Availability Attack	
10	WPA attack	3
11	WPA migration attack	3
12	Mdk3 Michael shutdown	2
13	Beacon flooding	3
	Total	**11/12**
	Authentication Attack	
14	Authentication Dos	3
15	Association flooding	3
	Total	**6/6**

The study has successfully done for each type of attack. Table 4 summarized the results for the identified area, and Table 5 represented the percentage of security testing. For the area access control and authentication attacks, with a result of 100%, we found that the system meets the guideline requirement and helps immensely in building a secured wirelessintrusion-detection system. Meanwhile, testing the security in the area of confidentiality and availability, with a result of 83% and 92% respectively, shown the system meets the guideline requirement and helps to build a good wireless intrusion-detection system. Hence, it proved that, these types of signature attack can easily recognize by the RaspyAir. On the other hand, the percentage for integrity attack was 75%, showed that this type of attack cannot easily be detected by RaspyAir. This is most probably because this type of attack used different type of parameter from the RaspyAir system.

Table 5: Percentage of the security testing

Attack Types	Score	Percentage
Access Control	9/9	100%
Integrity	9/12	75%
Confidentiality	5/6	83%
Availability	11/12	92%
Authentication	6/6	100%
Overall Percentage		88.89%

Table 5 shows the overall percentage was 88.89%, and it described that the RaspyAir followed the security guidelines and can be deployed on the wireless environment.

Table 6: Electricity consumption for both devices

	HP Compaq Notebook	Raspberry Pi
Electricity consumption (kWh)	0.0419	0.0045
Electricity cost (RM)	0.01	0.00

For the second testing, which is electricity consumption testing, found that the electricity consumption for Raspberry Pi which is 0.0045 kW was lower than HP Compaq Notebook, which is 0.0419 kW. Moreover, the electricity cost in two hours period for Raspberry Pi also lower than HP Compaq Notebook. Table 6 shows the electricity cost and consumption for both devices.

Conclusion

In this paper, we have presented the RaspyAir for home/work wireless environment. The system was specifically developed for monitoring the wireless intrusion detection for personal computer. The system used Raspberry Pi as an external tool to enhance the security performance of the personal computer. The used of Raspbery Pi and the RaspyAir system provide most economical and enhance the security performance for wireless intrusion detection. The advantage of RaspyAir due to the system is installed in an external tool and if anything happened, it will not harm the personal computer directly. Hence, the system provides a convenience way of monitoring the security level through the use of Raspberry Pi. Besides, the RaspyAir was evaluated using WSAM guideline and the result shown the RaspyAir followed the security guidelines and can be deployed on the wireless environment. Additionally, the electricity consumption of the RaspyAir was proved nine times saved than HP Compaq Notebook, likewise, the electricity cost for Raspberry Pi. The result of all criteria that was evaluated indicated that the RaspyAircontributes significantly in monitoring system for wireless intrusion detection for personal computer.

References

Agrawal, N., & Singhal, S. (2015). Smart drip irrigation system using raspberry pi and arduino. In *2015 International Conference on Computing, Communication Automation (ICCCA)* (pp. 928–932).

Aspernäs, A., & Simonsson, T. (2015). *IDS on Raspberry Pi: A Performance Evaluation*. Diploma thesis, University of Delaware.

Dmitry, S. K., & Dennis, Y. G. (2008). Network traffic analysis optimization for signature-based intrusion detection systems. In *Proceedings of the Spring/Summer Young Researchers' Colloquium on Software Engineering*.

Höfig, E., & Coşkun, H. (2009). Intrinsic monitoring using behaviour models in ipv6 networks. In *IEEE International Workshop on Modelling Autonomic Communications Environments* (pp. 86–99).

ICT Data and Statistics Division. (2015). *ICT Facts & Figures The World in 2015*. Retrieved from https://www.itu.int/en/ITU-D/Statistics/Documents/facts/ICTFactsFigures2015.pdf

Jia, C., & Chen, D. (2009). Performance evaluation of a collaborative intrusion detection system. In *2009 Fifth International Conference on Natural Computation* (Vol. 6, pp. 409–413).

Karthik, P. (2015). *Wireless Security Assessment Methodology* (Whitepaper) (pp. 1–7). Retrieved from ww.happiestminds.com/whitepapers/Wireless-Security-Assessment-Methodology.pdf

Makanju, A., Zincir-Heywood, N., & Milios, E. (2008). Adaptabilty of a GP Based IDS on Wireless Networks. In *Availability, Reliability and Security, 2008. ARES 08. Third International Conference on* (pp. 310–318).

Mingqiang, Z., Hui, H., & Qian, W. (2012). A graph-based clustering algorithm for anomaly intrusion detection. In *Computer Science & Education (ICCSE), 2012 7th International Conference on* (pp. 1311–1314).

Mo, Y., Ma, Y., & Xu, L. (2008). Design and implementation of intrusion detection based on mobile agents. In *IT in Medicine and Education, 2008. ITME 2008. IEEE International Symposium on* (pp. 278–281).

Paramanathan, A., Pahlevani, P., Thorsteinsson, S., Hundeboll, M., Lucani, D. E., & Fitzek, F. H. P. (2014). Sharing the Pi: Testbed Description and Performance Evaluation of Network Coding on the Raspberry Pi. In *2014 IEEE 79th Vehicular Technology Conference (VTC Spring)* (pp. 1–5).

Soetedjo, A., Ashari, M. I., Mahmudi, A., & Nakhoda, Y. I. (2014). Raspberry Pi based laser spot detection. In *2014 International Conference on Electrical Engineering and Computer Science (ICEECS)* (pp. 7–11).

Song, G. (2012). The study and design of network traffic monitoring based on socket. In *Computational and Information Sciences (ICCIS), 2012 Fourth International Conference on*(pp. 845–848).

Zargar, S. T., Joshi, J., & Tipper, D. (2014). DiCoTraM: A distributed and coordinated DDoS flooding attack tailored traffic monitoring. In *Information Reuse and Integration (IRI), 2014 IEEE 15th International Conference on*(pp. 120–129).

Article 6

Autonomous Robot Navigation Using Sense-Plan-Act (SPA) Approach

Nur Izyan Nazihah Abdul Rahim, Nurzaid Muhd Zain, Zulfikri Paidi
Faculty of Computer & Mathematical Sciences
Universiti Teknologi MARA Perlis Branch

Muhammad Luqman Muhd Zain
Faculty of Electrical & Automation Engineering Technology
TATi University College, Terengganu

Abstract

A mobile robot requires a good navigation system to travel around autonomously without bumping into any obstacles that either comes in its path (i.e. moving obstacle) or stands in its path (i.e. static obstacle). The main purpose of this project is to build a mobile robot and test its functionality so that it has the ability to avoid obstacles. The objectives are to build a prototype mobile robot, program the robot to become autonomous, and finally analyse its behaviour. The prototype robot was built using Arduino components. Meanwhile, the navigation system was developed using Sense-Plan-Act (SPA) approach. Infrared (IR) sensor and ultrasonic (US) sensor were used to provide robot's sensing ability. For each type of sensor, different experiments were conducted using three types of material that were used as the obstacles, which are the mirror, white surface and transparent glass. All the behaviours of the mobile robot were observed and recorded. From the results obtained, it shows that the US sensor was able to detect all material types of obstacles and the mobile robot successfully avoided the obstacles. Meanwhile, the IR sensor was only able to detect mirror and white surface. Through this experiment, it has also revealed that IR sensor was only able to detect transparent glass within short distances and this had caused the mobile robot to bump onto the obstacle while trying to change its direction.

Keywords: navigation system, collision avoidance, sensor, obstacle

Introduction

An autonomous mobile robot can travel around freely in an environment without having initial information of its surrounding. Since the robot can travel around freely from one point to another, it must have the ability to avoid obstacles that may block its way. Collision avoidance is a type of navigation method where a decision to avoid an obstacle is made after detecting an obstacle (Abiyev, Ibrahim & Erin, 2010). To control the mobile robot movement, a decision whether to turn right or to turn left requires a navigating strategy. One of the navigation strategies is the SPA approach. This approach is most suitable to use as control architecture to solve the problem of collision avoidance navigation especially if the obstacles are static. The SPA approach consisting of three linear steps (Gat, 1998). First, the presence of an obstacle is detected by sensor. Second, information collected from sensor is used to decide the next action that needs to be done. Lastly, mobile robot will act mechanically to avoid the obstacle. Two of the commonly used sensors that are used to calculate the distances between mobile robot and the obstacles are the Infrared (IR) sensor and the Ultrasonic (US) sensor.

i. IR Sensor

IR sensor is widely available, inexpensive and more practical because of its faster response time and narrower beam width (Gavrilut, Tiponut, Gacsadi & Tepelea, 2008; Mohammad, 2009; Adarsh, Mohamed Kaleemuddin, Dinesh & Ramachandran, 2016). Mohammad (2009) added that in IR sensor, phototransistor is used to detect the reflected light from the infrared Light Emitting Diode (LED) and it depends on the energy emitted from LED and the detectable range of the phototransistor.

IR sensors have the non-linear characteristics, thus need several parameters to detect light intensity. Those parameters are the surface reflectance properties, distance of sensor to the surface and the relative orientation of the emitter, detector and surface (Gavrilut et al., 2008). There are many papers that proposed the use of IR sensors for autonomous mobile robot navigation (Gat, 1998; Gavrilut et al., 2008; Rusu & Birou, 2010; Hajer, Mohamed & Mohamed, 2016). Nevertheless, since the IR sensors require knowing several parameters for distance measure, this has caused limited use of IR sensor in detecting the presence or absence of objects.

ii. US Sensor

According to Mohammad (2009), US sensor uses sound waves to detect the distance of an object that is located in front of the sensor. Adarsh et al., (2016) added that US sensor will transmit frequency sound waves that are generated, and evaluate the received echoes. The time interval between sent and receive signal will determine the distance of an obstacle or an object (Mohammad, 2009; Adarsh et al., 2016). Moreover, US sensors claimed to be a reliable source of obstacles detections where they can be used even in condition of poor lighting and transparent objects (Benet, Blanes, Simó, & Pérez, 2002). US sensors however have few limitations due to their wide beam-width, sensitivity to mirror-like surfaces and the inability to recognize objects within certain distance (Mohammad, 2009; Adarsh et al., 2016). Therefore, for that reasons, only reflecting objects that are almost normal to the sensor acoustic axis may be accurately detected.

Methodology

The development of this project was divided into two main parts, which were assembling the hardware components and creating the programming for SPA approach. Both parts play an important role in completing this project. The table below shows the required hardware and software components for this research project.

Table 1: Hardware and Software Components

Requirements	Components
Hardware	Arduino UNO Microcontroller Wheels DC Motor Motor Driver Acrylics Power Source Monochrome Terminal Solderless Connectors Sensors (IR and US)
Software	Arduino IDE Arduino Language Programming Algorithm

i. Assembling Hardware Components

To assemble the hardware components, circuit diagram was created. Circuit diagram is a simplified conventional graphical representation of an electrical circuit. There are four circuit diagrams created for this project:

1) Motor to Motor Driver Circuit
2) Motor Driver to Arduino UNO Microcontroller Circuit
3) IR Sensors to Arduino UNO Microcontroller Circuit
4) US Sensor to Arduino UNO Microcontroller Circuit

The final product of the assembled mobile robot is shown in Figure 1 below.

Figure 1: Mobile Robot

ii. Programming the Mobile Robot

In this phase, we have created programs for the navigation system of the mobile robot. The programs were written using Arduino programming language and are called Sketch. For the purpose of this project, Sketches were created based on the algorithms developed for mobile robot with IR sensors and mobile robot with US sensor as depicted in Figure 2.

iii. Experimentation

In this phase, the mobile robot was released in the environment with static obstacles. The obstacles in the environment were made of three material types, which are mirror, white surface and transparent glass. As mentioned in the previous section, two main experiments were conducted in this project based on the algorithm designed for mobile robot with IR sensors and US sensor as shown in Figure 2.

For the first experiment, the mobile robot with IR sensor received signal inputs from three IR sensors that were placed at the front, left and right side of the mobile robot. The mobile robot was released to travel autonomously in the environment where obstacles were placed and observation on the behaviour of the mobile robot was recorded.

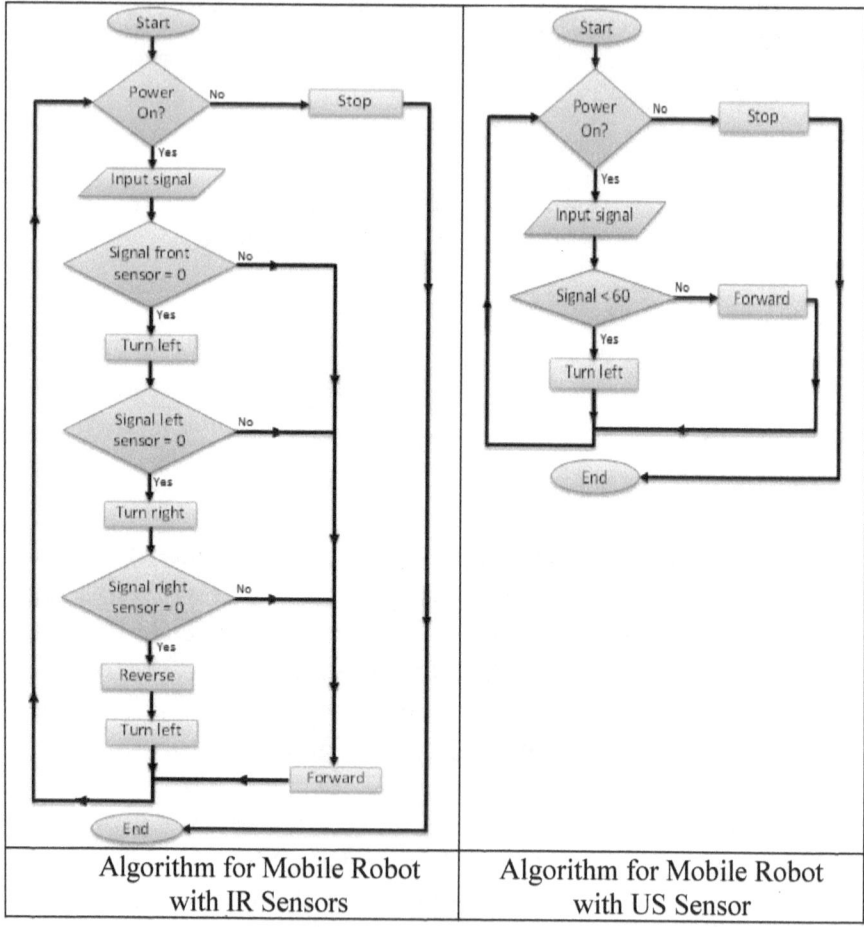

Algorithm for Mobile Robot with IR Sensors	Algorithm for Mobile Robot with US Sensor

Figure 2: Flowcharts of Algorithm for Mobile Robot Sensors

Meanwhile, for the second experiment that involved mobile robot with US sensor, it requires only one US sensor and the sensor was placed at the front of the mobile robot. The mobile robot was then released to travel autonomously in the environment with obstacles. The behaviour of the mobile robot was also observed and recorded.

Results and Analysis

i. Experiment 1: Mobile Robot with IR sensors
In this experiment, the sensing ranges of IR sensor towards the material types of obstacle were also recorded as depicted in Figure 3. Based on Figure 3, the IR sensor was able to detect mirror at 12cm range, which is the farthest range. Meanwhile, it has also revealed that IR sensor placed on the mobile robot could only detect the transparent glass within a short range only, in this case as close as 2cm range.

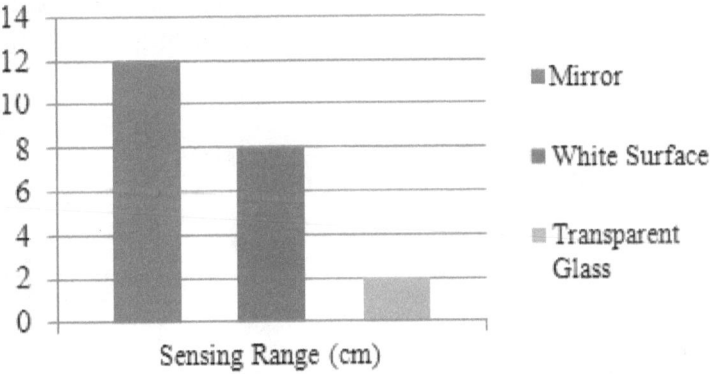

Figure 3: Sensing ranges of the IR sensor towards the material types

Further investigation of mobile robot's behaviours with IR sensors was recorded. Table 2 below shows the summary of the behavior towards the three obstacles.

Table 2: Summary of Behaviour of Mobile Robot with IR sensors

Material Types of Obstacles	Behaviour of Mobile Robot
Mirror	• Mobile robot was able to avoid obstacle and navigate smoothly in the environment.
White Surface	• Mobile robot was able to avoid obstacle and navigate smoothly in the environment.
Transparent Glass	• Mobile robot bumped to obstacle glass while changing direction to left. • Reason: distance between mobile robot and obstacle was too close, this had caused delayed for the mobile robot to make decisions.

From Table 2, it was revealed that mobile robot with IR sensors could navigate smoothly in the environment that had mirror and white surface as the obstacles. Meanwhile, this experiment has also revealed that the mobile robot failed to avoid the transparent glass as the sensing range was too close, causing the mobile robot to bump onto the obstacle.

To justify these findings, we have analysed the situations regarding all the three obstacles as mentioned in Table 3 below.

Table 3: Analysis of Material Types of Obstacle

Material Types of Obstacles	Analysis
Mirror	• Mirror has silver surface. Light cannot travel through the silver, but the silver also cannot absorb the light. As a result, the light reflected of the surface of the silver. • Mirror image is an example of specular reflection. Specular reflection is defined as light reflected from a smooth surface at a definite angle. So, mirror does not scatter lights.

| White Surface | • When light emits to white surface, the lights reflected back. The light reflects in all the directions, called diffuse reflection. White objects have very rough bumpy surfaces. This causes scattering of lights. |
| Transparent Glass | • Light travel through the glass because there is no surface that reflects the light. However,only some of the light reflected back to and this caused delay for the sensor detect the obstacle. |

ii. Experiment 2: Mobile Robot with US sensor

Meanwhile, in the second experiment with the mobile robot attached with the US sensor, it has revealed that the US sensor was able to detect all obstacles accurately and had caused the mobile robot to navigate smoothly in the environment.

This is due to the fact that mirror, white surface and transparent glass completely reflects back the ultrasonic waves. Other materials such as cloth, cotton and wool would be difficult for the US sensor to detect because these type of materials would absorb the ultrasonic waves. Table 4 below explained the behaviours of the mobile robot with US sensor used in this experiment.

Table 4: Summary of Behaviour of Mobile Robot with US sensor

Position of Obstacles	Behaviour of Mobile Robot
Front	• Mobile robot turned left after detected obstacle at front (sensor produced signal input less than 60) and moving forward after no obstacle was detected.
Front & Left	• Mobile robot continuously turned left as long as the sensor detects obstacles. Mobile robot move forward only after sensor produce signal input more than 60 (no obstacle).

Conclusion

In conclusion, the behaviour of mobile robot is highly depending on the type of sensor and material types of the obstacle that is use. Both IR sensor and US sensor has its pros and cons. For instance, IR sensor is simple and inexpensive and it works by emits and reflects infrared light. The drawback to this sensor is that light does not reflect the same way off every surface. Thus, the readings will be different depending on the types of surface, colours and shades. Furthermore, this sensor also cannot work accurately if there is direct or indirect sunlight. Therefore, IR sensor is not suitable to use for outdoor application.

On the other hand, US sensor provides more accurate reading than IR sensor since this sensor produces analog signal that calculates the distance range between object and the sensor. Nonetheless, a drawback of ultrasonic sensor is on the distance reading. To obtain an adequate picture of the environment around the mobile robot, many sensors must be used together. US sensors use sound waves for ranging, so it can be used outside in bright sunlight, but the waves may be thrown off by a sound absorbing obstacle, like a sponge.

For future research, it is recommended to combine the use of IR sensor and US sensor on the mobile robot. Additionally, to ensure the reliability of the mobile robot's navigation system, more experiments on the test plan must be done. The mobile robot should be released in an environment with variety of obstacles' condition such as zigzag path and obstacles that are place randomly in a space.

References

Abiyev, R., Ibrahim, D. & Erin, B. (2010). Navigation of mobile robots in the presence of obstacles, *Advances in Engineering Software*, 41(10–11), pp. 1179-1186, 2010.

Adarsh, S., Mohamed Kaleemuddin, S., Dinesh Bose Ramachandran, K. (2016). Performance comparison of Infrared and Ultrasonic sensors for obstacles of different materials in vehicle/ robot navigation applications. *IOP Conf. Series: Materials Science and Engineering 149*, 012141 doi:10.1088/1757-899X/149/1/012141.

Benet G. Blanes, F. Simó, J. E. & Pérez, P. (2002). Using infrared sensors for distance measurement in mobile robots. Robotics and autonomous systems. Robotics *and autonomous systems*, 40(4), pp. 255-266.

Gat, E. (1998). *On Three-Layer Architectures*, Artificial intelligence and mobile robots, pp. 195-210, MIT Press Cambridge, MA, USA.

Gavrilut, I., Tiponut, V., Gacsadi, A. & Tepelea, L. (2008). Wall-following Method for an Autonomous Mobile Robot using Two IR Sensors. *12th WSEAS International Conference on SYSTEMS*, pp. 205-209.

Hajer, O., Mohamed, S. M. & Mohamed, M. (2016). Fuzzy Logic Based Control for Autonomous Mobile Robot Navigation. Computational Intelligence and Neuroscience, Volume 2016, Article ID 9548482, 10 pages http://dx.doi.org/10.1155/2016/9548482.

Mohammad, T. (2009). Using Ultrasonic and Infrared Sensors for Distance Measurement, *International Journal of Mechanical, Aerospace, Industrial, Mechatronic and Manufacturing Engineering*, Vol.3, No.3, pp. 267 – 272.

Rusu, C.G. & Birou, I.T (2010). Obstacle Avoidance Fuzzy System for Mobile Robot with IR Sensors, *10th International Conference On Development And Application Systems*, pp. 25 – 29.

SECTION III:

INFORMATION TECHNOLOGY
&
SYSTEM SCIENCES

Article 7

Designing an Augmented Reality in-car Driving Simulator

Haryati Fauzi, Aznoora Osman, Muhamad Arif Hashim
Faculty of Computer & Mathematical Sciences
Universiti Teknologi MARA Cawangan Perlis

Ahmad Hanif Ahmad Baharin
Institute of Visual Informatics
Universiti Kebangsaan Malaysia,

(This project is funded by the Ministry of Higher Education Malaysia through research grant RAGS/1/2014/ICT02/UITM//3)

Abstract - This paper demonstrates the design of augmented reality (AR) in-car driving simulator system architecture and its experimental design. AR in-car driving simulator is developed in order to explore its effect towards subjects' simulator sickness when operating the driving simulator. Sensory conflict theory postulates that simulator sickness is a condition where an information between vestibular input system and visual that provides orientation and movement information is misaligned. Simulator sickness is a well-known issue entangled with simulator and various past research revealed that some of the methods to avoid simulator sickness are by taking prescribed medicine, shortening the length of drives and adjusting light of driving simulation environment. Augmented reality allows a combination between real world views with computer-generated object and runs in a real-time performance. By using AR, it is possible to create an outdoor driving simulator that allows a real world view with a mixture of case study that been replicate by computer. Affording similar driving experience to driving a normal car, AR is believed to be an alternative solution to simulator sickness. Therefore, the AR driving simulator would be employed in experimental study to measure its effect on simulator sickness towards subjects.

Keywords: driving simulator, augmented reality, simulator sickness, experimental design, system architecture

Introduction

Driving simulator can be defined as a machine that supplies a realistic impersonation of an operation of a vehicle that is used to study driving behaviour, discover solutions for driving issues and assisting a completion of interior and exterior designs (Hale & Stanney, 2014). According to (Medenica, Kun, Paek, & Palinko,

2011), driver's attention escalates if more realistic driving simulator environment is provided. Even with the existence of new sensor technologies, high-end display and computer graphics software that allows a creation of virtual environment closed to real environment, the simulator sickness issues still exist. Sensory conflicts theory defines simulator sickness as a mismatch of communication between vestibular input systems and visual that provides an information of orientation and movement information (Domeyer, Cassavaugh, & Backs, 2013).

In essence, driving simulator shows a movement of virtual environment on display but the subject's body does not register any movement, which in turn creates a conflict that leads to simulator sickness. However, it is believed that simulator sickness can be avoided if the driving simulator is moving along with subject, similar to driving a normal car, this condition is possible if a driving simulator simulation is developed using AR concept. Therefore, AR in-car driving simulator system architecture is designed to illustrate the operational view of driving simulator. Also, the research design has been thoroughly outlined to ensure smooth and ethically sound experiment.

Designing and Development of the AR in-car driving simulator

i. Hardware and software specification

Hardware specification for driving simulator consists of three (3) basic components, which are AR glasses, camera and a car. A car is required because it is an outdoor type of driving simulator, and a car with an automatic gear is chosen because it is much easier for subject to concentrate to the experiment matters and not everyone has the ability to drive a manual gear car. A camera is installed in the car to record subject behaviour during the experiment. Subject behaviour is collected as an additional data to the experiment. As for AR glasses, ODG R-7 Glasses (AR glasses) is chosen. This glasses powered by Qualcomm Snapdragon 805, 2.7 GHz quad-core processor, 3GB pop LP-DDR3 RAM and 64GB storage. It is also equipped with dual

720p stereoscopic see-through displays at up to 80 frames-per-seconds (fps), 60 percent see-through transmission and magnetic removable photochromic lens. This AR glasses also consists sensors including altitude sensor, humidity sensor, ambient light sensor and multiple integrated inertial measuring unit (accelerometer, gyroscope and magnetometer) sensor. As for input and output system, two (2) digital microphones (user and environment), magnetic charging port with USB on-the-go and magnetic stereo audio ports with ear buds are supplied. One of the reason this glasses is chosen because no cords needed-sensors, processors, displays and power are all self-contained.

For the development process, a computer will be used, which powered by Intel ® Core ™ i5-4690 CPU @ 3.50 GHZ, 4GB of RAM, 64-bit operating system with x64 based processor, and using Windows 10 Pro. On the other hand, 3D Max 2016 software is used to develop 3d models and Unity 5.4.xx with Vuforia plugin is used to develop the AR environment that will used in the driving simulator.

ii. System Architecture
Figure 1 illustrates the system architecture of AR in-car driving simulator that includes all hardware needed for the driving simulator to operate efficiently. Subject will take a position on a driver seat in the AR in-car driving simulator. Subject will be wearing an AR glasses, which is used to collect data and to display graphics. This interaction will be initiated once subject starts driving. When there is a movement of the driving simulator, the trackers (position tracker and orientation tracker) on the AR glasses worn by subject will send a tracker data pattern to process the transformation of view pattern.

Based on location and direction data provided, three-dimension (3D) geometry is transformed using transformation matrices to produce a 3D object that aligns with the real world view. OpenGL then will render the information and projecting the result to the glasses display. Subject will response based on the information being projected to the AR glasses display. A camera, which is installed in the car will be used as monitoring and recording tool of the subjects' behaviour and response during the experiment. This data will be treated as a secondary data.

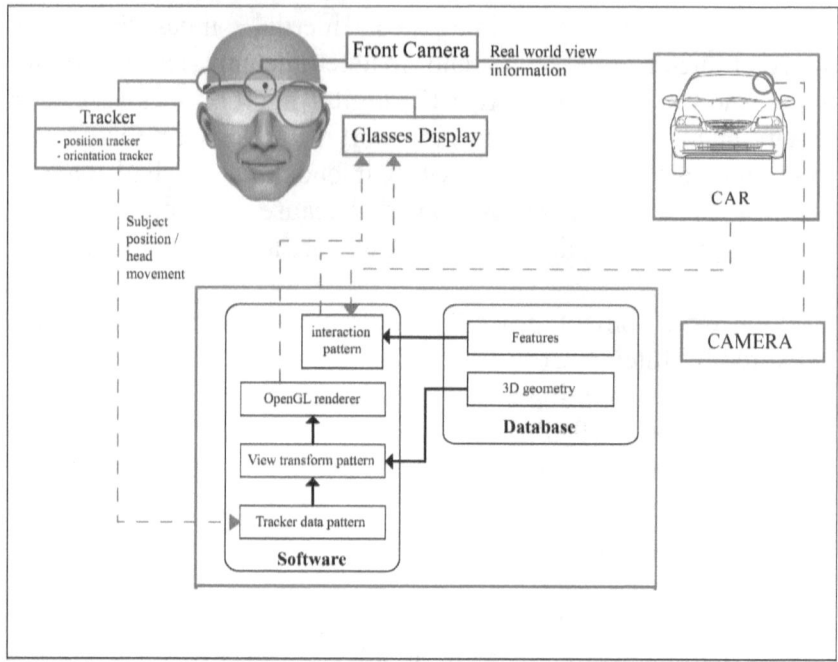

Figure 1: System Architecture of AR in-car Driving Simulator

Experimental Design

i. Screening the potential subject

To select subject for this research, subject will undergo a screening process. Screening process is important to determine if an individual is qualified to participate in this research. Potential subject may fill a form via printed copy or online, and their general information such as name, age, race, address, phone number(s) and information of their health will be collected. Persons having illness related to heart, brain, visual (other than corrected vision), inner ear ailments and pregnant women are not eligible to participate. There is an exception on subject whom had a farsightedness vision and nearsightedness vision if glasses or contact lens is worn during experiment session. Those who have inner ear ailments are not qualified because deaf individual cannot have the sense of motion sickness (Hain, 2016). Age range of preferred subject is between 21 and 55 years old, and with at least two (2) years of driving experiences. Confirming given information by potential subject by phone are exclusionary for the research, and thus a visit to the site would be a waste of time.

ii. Instruments used in experimental design

A consent form, demographic questionnaire and Motion Sickness History Questionnaire (MSHQ) will be distributed to subject prior to any experimental sessions. The Simulator Sickness Questionnaire (SSQ) (Kennedy, Lane, Berbaum, & Lilienthal, 1993) were administered to obtain measure of dependent variables, which is simulator sickness. A consent form is a basic document that needs to be signed by subject to confirm that a mutual agreement has been achieved and subject is aware of the risk that might be involved during the experiment. MSHQ was developed as subjective motion sickness measurement (Reason & Brand, 1975 as cited in Moss, 2008). The MSHQ purpose is to acquire a measurement of subject exposure's frequency to particular type of transportation that leads to the occurrence of motion sickness. The result of MSHQ is a solitary merit indicating susceptibility to motion sickness. SSQ on the other hand, will be measuring the severity level of simulator sickness exposure to subject. SSQ consists 16 items and four scale that represents the severity scale as none, slight, moderate or severe and obtaining a score of '0', '1', '2' and '3'.

iii. Experimental design

It is important to have an experimental design before commencement of any experiment. Driving simulator often has many input factors and determining a significant impact on performance measures or response of interest, which can be a truly intimidating task. Figure 2 shows the flow of experimental design for this study.

Once subject arrives at experiment site, subject will be briefed on the research introduction, objectives and experimental task within the experiment site. If the subject agree to proceed with the experiment, subject needs to sign consign form, confirming the general information that has been collected during screening period, and complete the MSHQ. Subject will be trained to operate the AR in-car driving simulator and explained how to complete the experiment. Subject needs to do practice for two minutes with the AR in-car driving simulator to be familiar with the test environment before actual experiment begins. Subject will start the experiment once they are ready. At any point in the experiment, subject has the right to rest, stop and discontinue should they experience sickness. Once the experiment is completed, subject needs to complete SSQ and be advised not to drive for the next half an hour to avoid any incident. They will be provided with refreshments and receive a payment as a complimentary for their participation.

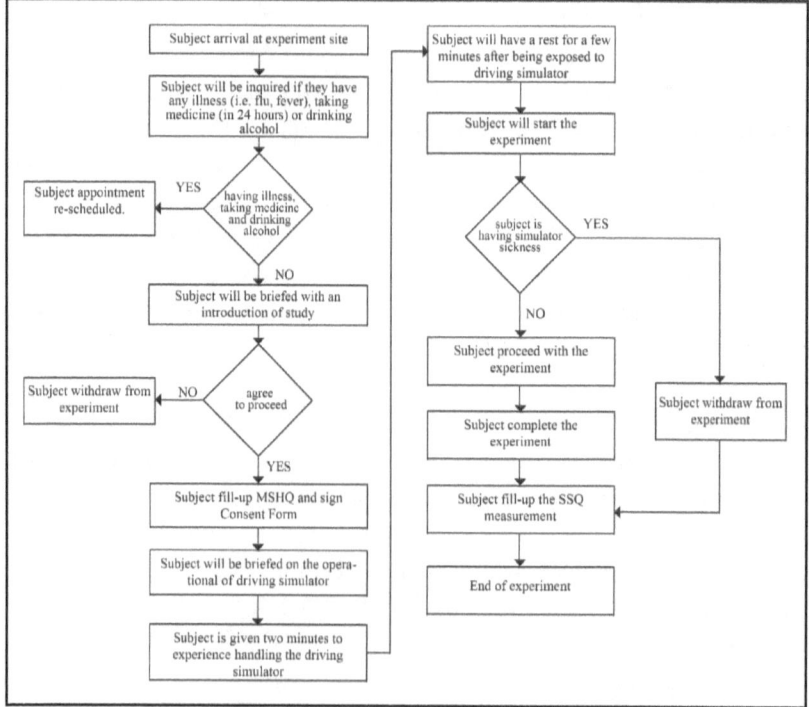

Figure 2: Experimental design

Conclusion

This paper shows the system architecture and experimental design for the AR in-car driving simulator. This design can be employed easily and helpful to support the AR in-car driving simulator experiments. In the future, the driving simulator will be used as a platform to experiment with more complex scenario for investigating various case study including a test for new technology, driver behaviour, engineering counter measure or a driving crash risks and hazard.

References

Domeyer, J. E., Cassavaugh, N. D., & Backs, R. W. (2013). The use of adaptation to reduce simulator sickness in driving assessment and research. *Accident Analysis and Prevention*, 53, 127-132.

Hain, T. C. (2016, May 27). Motion Sickness. Retrieved from http://www.dizziness-and balance.com/disorders/central/motion.htm

Hale, K. S., & Stanney, K. M. (2014). *Handbook of virtual environments: Design,*.

Kennedy, R. S., Lane, N. E., Berbaum, K. S., & Lilienthal , M. G. (1993). Simulator sickness questionnaire: An enhanced method for quantifying simulator sickness. *International journal of aviation psychology*, 203-220.

Medenica, Z., Kun, A., Paek, T., & Palinko, O. (2011). Augmented reality vs. street views: A driving simulator study comparing two emerging navigation aids.

Moss, J. D. (2008). Characteristics of Head Mounted Displays and their Effects on Simulator Sickness.

Osterhout Design Group. (2016, 10 25). R-7 Smartglasses. Retrieved from Osterhout Group: http://www.osterhoutgroup.com/products-r7-glasses

Reason , J. T., & Brand, J. J. (1975). *Motion Sickness*. London: Academic.

Article 8

Enhanced Collaborative E-learning for Programming Using Open Learner Model

Mahfudzah Othman, Siti Hana Quzaima Alias, Nur Fajrina Mohd Rashidi
Faculty of Computer & Mathematical Sciences,
Universiti Teknologi MARA Perlis Branch

Abstract
Open learner model is mainly used to depict learner's achievements and progress in particular subject using variety of qualitative representations ranging from simple representations such as skill meters to more complex Bayesian network models. Currently, open learner models are only available for individual learners and mostly used separately from e-Learning systems. Therefore, this paper proposed an enhanced model of collaborative e-learning by integrating open learner model that will represent students' achievements and milestones while learning introductory programming course. The aim is to produce learner models using graphical skill meters that are not only used to reflect individual performances, but also a group of learners' academic achievements and milestones. Through this, learners will be able to reflect their own performances in introductory programming subject and become more engaged and responsible towards their own progress.

Keywords: *programming; e-learning, collaborative; open learner model*

Introduction

Introductory programming courses are allegedly one of the most challenging courses among the first year students in Computer Science field (Yadin, 2011). The average passing mark for this subject was recorded at only at 67 percent in fifteen different countries all around the globe including United States, United Kingdom, Indonesia and Australia (Watson & Li, 2014).

The complexity of the programming subject itself that resemblances engineering activities with high demands of intellectual capabilities becomes the most apparent reason for the high failure rates in the subject (Valentin et al., 2013). Other factors involved the complexity of the programming languages used, the lack of interest and motivation in learning programming and variations in teaching and learning styles and strategies (Kalelioglu & Gulbahar, 2014).

In order to improve students' performance in introductory programming course, recent studies have showed many usages of information and communication technologies (ICT) such as multimedia courseware, interactive games, mobile applications and e-learning systems (Tsai et al., 2011). Meanwhile, with the emergence of the Internet and e-learning platforms, collaborative e-learning systems have been seen as potential efforts to increase learners' interests, engagements, communications and collaborations especially to support distance learning activities. Previous studies include the developments of Supporting Collaboration and Adaptation in a Learning Environment (SCALE), Programming Assignment aSsessment System (PASS) and AutoLEP (Verginis et al., 2011; Wang et al., 2011; Law et al., 2010).

Nevertheless, most of these collaborative e-learning platforms do not provide users with the open learner models; models that help to visualize learners' achievements, milestones and even problematic areas in certain subjects. Furthermore, most of the open learner models are often developed and used separately with the e-learning systems. In addition, these open learner models are also usually used to cater individual learners (Bull & Kay, 2007).

Therefore, this paper will propose an enhanced model of collaborative e-learning system that is integrated with open learner models. This system will support not only individual learners but also groups of learners. The aim is for the learners to be more engaged with their own performance as well as their groups' achievements in introductory programming course.

Open learner models used in the system will support the idea of self-assessment and self-regulated learning, reflect their milestones and marked their problematic areas in certain topics in the introductory programming course.

Related Works

i. Collaborative e-learning system for programming

Collaborative e-learning system is rapidly changing the landscape of our education system. Most of the features of typical e-learning systems were enhanced in order to support groups' collaborations and discussions over the Internet. This concept is famously being described as computer-supported social learning (CSSL) system that offers support to foster groups' communication and collaborative activities (Halimi et al., 2011).

In learning programming, several collaborative e-learning systems have been developed such as the COLLEGE that stands for COLLaborative Edition, compilinG and Execution of programs that facilitates the collaborations and communications between students. It is also aimed to improve students' cognitive abilities and motivations (Chang & Chen, 2008). Other than that, a project named EduJudge has been constructed to integrate with the UVA Online Judge, which is an existing online programming trainer. It is aimed to provide an educational environment that supports collaborations among teachers and students in terms of providing automated evaluation systems, interactive communications and helping to improve students' motivation (Verdú et al., 2012).

Recent study has also showed the use of collaborative online problem solving with computer games to improve students' metacognitive skills, engagements and motivations in learning computer programming (Bernard & Bachu, 2015). Other than that, one project named as Protus 2.1 is being developed to provide recommendation in programming tutoring system by applying collaborative tagging (Vesin et al., 2016). The advance intelligent tutoring system that is used to learn basic concepts in Java programming will direct learners' activities and recommends relevant actions, thus improving students' interests and engagements (Vesin et. al, 2016).

ii. Open learner model and collaborative e-learning

According to Bull and Kay (2007), there are two types of open learner model visual representations that can be used to represent learners' achievements, which are the simple or complex learner model. Simple learner models will normally present simple skill meters that display learner's level of knowledge, difficulties and learning process for every selected topic (Bull & Kay, 2007). In the other hand, the complex learner models will use varieties of modeling techniques such as knowledge tracing in cognitive modeling or Bayesian networks to present information that is more detailed to the learners (Bull & Kay, 2007).

Up until today, not many researches have been done in developing open learner models that support online collaborations. They are mainly being developed for individual learners and often separated from the e-learning systems. For instance, one project that combines open learner model with a competence-based feedback for collaborative language learning done by Kickmeier-Rust et al. (2014) or helping to scaffold students' reflection towards collaborative brainstorming by Clayphan et al. (2014). Moreover, Alotaibi and Bull (2012) have also used the Facebook with the open learner model named OLMlets to investigate the effectiveness of online collaboration and learner's interactions.

Proposed Model of an Enhanced Collaborative e-Learning with Open Learner Model

The proposed model as depicted in Figure 3 represents new elements that are integrated in the enhanced collaborative e-learning system for programming. As shown in Figure 3, the enhanced factors for the proposed system include collaboration concepts and open learner model. To begin the collaborative activities, firstly, the collaborative groups were formed. In this case, the lecturers have to assign the collaborative group members and upload the collaborative activities such as online quizzes in the e-learning system. Using the concept of collaboration, the online quizzes were done in groups where the group members communicate via the Web 2.0 tools provided in the system such as the chat rooms or forums.

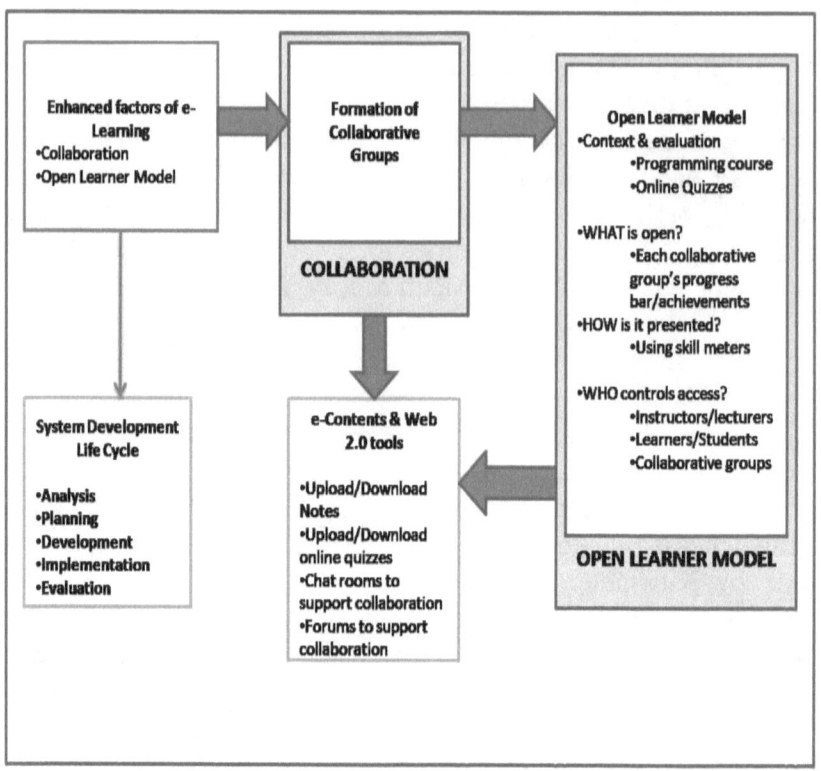

Figure 3: Model of an Enhanced Collaborative e-Learning for Programming with Open Learner Model

Meanwhile, for the open learner model, the Student Models that Invite the Learner In (SMILI) Framework is referred. Based on the framework, four parts were considered, where the first one was the context and evaluation. In this part, we have addressed the open learner suitability for the overall interaction and the types of assessments. For this project, the introductory programming course was selected and the online quizzes for each topic were developed. Two types of questions were created; multiple choice and short structured questions. For each type of questions, there are also six levels of cognitive development based on Bloom's Taxonomy cognitive domains. The levels are the knowledge, comprehension, application, analysis, synthesis and evaluation.

Next, we need to address the visibility of the open learner models in the system and the visual representations used for it. Considering the students have answered the online quizzes, the open learner models were presented for both individuals and collaborative groups. In this case, the simple visual representation using skill meters were developed. The skill meters will show three types of progress; the percentages of successfully answered, not successfully answered and not answered questions. Each individual can view their own open learner model for each topic in the course and their team members' open learner models. This idea is to encourage the learners to improve and motivate each other, thus, supporting engagements and team motivations.

Finally, the accessibility and control of the open learner models were also being considered. The enhanced collaborative e-learning system will provide method for the lecturers to evaluate and analyze learner models. Furthermore, the open learner models provided in the system are also interactive and change according to the learners' performances, thus, providing mechanisms for self-evaluation and self-regulated learning.

Conclusion
One of the advantages of using e-learning system is that it supports multi users from dispersed locations with less cost and few barriers. The enhanced collaborative e-learning system proposed in this paper, will not only support individual learning activities, but also provide mechanism to allow online collaborations and communications among group of students. Furthermore, this system also has a unique ability to represent learners' achievements in a form of visual representations called the open learner model. Individuals or collaborative groups are able to reflect their own progress and address their problematic topics in the introductory programming course by just referring to the open learner models.

The open learner model is not being used as definite marks for the students, because the aim is to allow the learners to reflect their performances and improve them from time to time. Therefore, the visibility, accessibility and changeability offered by the open learner models can be seen as one of the efforts to increase students' engagements and motivations in learning programming, thus, helping to improve their performance in this subject. Future research will involve the adaptive e-learning system with the open learner model plays an important role to make learning programming via online system more personalized.

References

Alotaibi, M & Bull, S. (2012). Combining Facebook and open learner models to encourage collaborative learning. Proc. of 20th ICCE Conference on Computer-supported Collaborative Learning (CSCL) and Learning Sciences, Singapore, pp. 71-75.

Bernard, M & Bachu, E. (2015). Enhancing the Metacognitive Skill of Novice Programmers Through Collaborative Learning. Metacognition: Fundaments, Applications, and Trends, Volume 76 of the series Intelligent Systems Reference Library, pp 277-298.

Bull, S. & Kay, J. (2007). Student models that invite the learner in: The SMILI open learner modelling framework, Int. Journal of Artificial Intelligence in Education, 17(2), pp. 89-120.

Chang, WC. & Chen, KC. (2008). Collaborative Learning Tool Applying to C Programming Language. ICWL '08 Proceedings of the 7th international conference on Advances in Web Based Learning, pp. 178–186.

Clayphan, A., Martinez-Maldonado, R., Kay, J. & Bull, S. (2014). Scaffolding reflection for collaborative brainstorming, in Trausan-Matu, S, Boyer, KE, Crosby, M, Panourgia, K, editors. Intelligent Tutoring Systems, Springer International Publishing, Switzerland, pp. 615-616.

Halimi, K., Seridi, H. & Faron-Zucker, C. (2011). Solearn: A social learning network, Proc. IEEE International Conference of Computational Aspects of Social Networks (CASoN), October 2011, pp.130 – 135.

Kalelioglu, F. & Gulbahar, Y. The effects of teaching programming via Scratch on problem solving skills: A discussion from learners' perspective, Informatics in Education, 13(1), 2014, pp. 33–50.

Kickmeier-Rust, M.D., Bull, S. & Meissl-Egghart, G. (2014). Collaborative language learning in immersive virtual worlds: Competence-based formative feedback and open learner modeling, International Journal of Serious Games, 1(2), 2014, pp. 67-74.

Law, K.M.Y., Lee, V.C.S & Yu, Y.T. (2010). Learning motivation in e-learning facilitated computer programming courses. Computers & Education, vol. 55, pp. 218–228.

Tsai, W.T., Wu, L., Elston, J. & Chen, Y.N. (2011). Collaborative learning using Wiki web sites for Computer Science undergraduate education: A case study. IEEE Trans. Edu., 54(1), pp. 114-124.

Valentin, L.F., Pardo, A. & Kloos, C.D. (2013). Addressing drop-out and sustained effort issues with large practical groups using an automated delivery and assessment system, Computers & Education, 61, pp. 33-42.

Verdú, E., Regueras, L.M., Verdú, M.J., Leal, J.P, de Castro, J.P & Queirós, R. (2012). A distributed system for learning programming on-line, Computers & Education, 58, pp. 1-10.

Verginis, I, Gogoulou, A., Gouli, E., Boubouka, M. & Grigoriadou, M. (2011). Enhancing learning in introductory computer sciences courses through SCALE: An empirical study. IEEE Trans. Edu., 54 (1), pp. 1-13.

Vesin, B., Klašnja-Milićević, A. & Ivanović, M. (2016). PROTUS 2.1: Applying Collaborative Tagging for Providing Recommendation in Programming Tutoring System, Advances in Web-Based Learning – ICWL 2016, Volume 10013 of the series Lecture Notes in Computer Science, pp 236-245.

Watson, C. & Li, F.W.B. (2014). Failure rates in introductory programming revisited, Proc. 2014 Conference on Innovation & Technology in Computer Science Education (ITiCSE '14), pp. 39-44.

Yadin, A. (2011). Reducing the dropout rate in an introductory programming courses, ACM inroads, 2 (4), pp. 71-76.

Article 9

An Evaluation on Personal Finance Web System for University Students

Nor Azzyati Hashim, Nor Faridah Bani Omar, Romiza Md Nor
Faculty of Computer & Mathematical Sciences,
Universiti Teknologi MARA Perlis Branch

Abstract

The exposure of personal finance literacy among youth has started to get further attention worldwide on account of economic instability and rising cost of living. Knowing about personal finance as early as possible becomes important because being fit in money management is one of the factors that lead for better lifestyle and early financial freedom. A web-based system in a university setting is expected to help university students take advantage of this opportunity. This paper investigates the benefits of a web system called e-Personal Finance (e-PF) for bachelor degree students in Universiti Teknologi MARA (UiTM) Perlis Branch. e-PF is composed of three main sections; Financial Test, Budget Planner and Finance Calculator. Evaluation for this web system using usability testing involved 50 bachelor degree students from seven faculties and two finance lecturers cooperated to give their expert point of view and opinion. From the findings, it is discovered that e-PF can help students to improve their knowledge and attitude about personal finance. As a conclusion, e-Personal Finance is found to be relevant in becoming one of education medium to assist university students in personal finance literacy, planning and management.

Keywords: personal finance, financial literacy, personal finance web system, usability testing, university students

Introduction

A fluctuation in economic stability and rising cost of living make personal finance becomes more crucial now than before. Seddon (2012) referred personal finance as "individuals and household consumption possibilities, both now and in the future, and is therefore driven by both income and wealth" and its distribution. Basically, the area of personal finance covers financial planning, money management, insurance protection and investments management (Keown, 2010). Due to broad area of personal finance, the exposure of at least the basic such as financial

---

planning and money management should be introduced at earlier age as possible.

When people are better informed about personal finance at younger age, they can develop improved financial literacy. Organisation for Economic Co-operation and Development (OECD) (2012) defined financial literacy as "knowledge and understanding of financial concepts, and the skills, motivation and confidence to apply such knowledge and understanding in order to make effective decisions across a range of financial contexts, to improve the financial well-being of individuals and society, and to enable participation in economic life." According to Chen and Lope (1998), university students who had low financial knowledge tend to make wrong financial opinion that could cause incorrect financial decision. That is why improving financial literacy among university students is important because their financial knowledge and practices during this time will significantly influence their financial situation after graduation (Cude et al., 2006).

In Malaysia, knowledge about personal finance among university students is still considered at minimum level. A study found that students did not have adequate and appropriate financial knowledge and skills concerning that many of them depended on education loan (Jariah et al., 2004). Another study revealed that students lack of financial literacy even on routine skills of money management (Ibrahim, et al., 2009). Furthermore, a research review on financial literacy among undergraduate students from four published studies in Malaysia has shown that lacking of financial knowledge requires national attention to provide financial literacy education to students (Ahsan, 2013).

There are many methods that can be used to offer financial literacy. Apart from seminars, pamphlets, newspapers, radio and television, informative website is considered as an efficient and cost-effective method to deliver information and educate about financial literacy (Toussaint-Comeau & Rhine, 2000; Cude,

2006). Thus, a web system development is applicable to achieve the purpose.

In light of the above, a web system called e-Personal Finance (e-PF) was developed to help university students to improve their financial knowledge and attitude that will lead to better financial literacy of financial planning and money management. Evaluation of a web system to measure its effectiveness, efficiency and satisfaction of users can be achieved with usability testing (ISO, 1998 as cited by Bevan, 2009; as cited by Hornbaek, 2006). For that reason, usability testing was conducted to evaluate e-PF web system.

Research Model
Figure 1 shows the research model that has been applied in the development of e-PF.

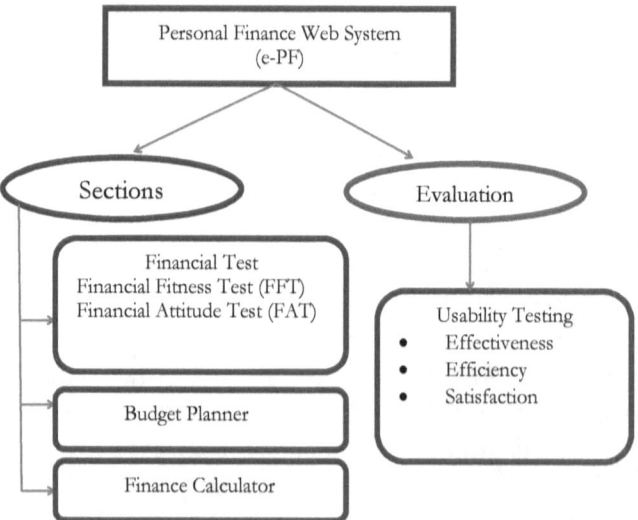

Figure 1: Research model for the development of e-PF.

e-PF focuses on three sections which are financial test, budget planner and finance calculator. Financial tests which were adapted from Financial Fitness Test (FFT) (Cameron et al, 2013) and Financial Attitude Test (FAT) (Ibrahim, 2009) to provide students evaluation about their financial knowledge and attitude.

Budget planner acts as a financial diary for students to improve on financial planning skills. It is developed in place of a financial diary for students to type their monthly income and anticipated expenditure. As for finance calculator, it can be used by students for money management. It is a tool to calculate the actual income and expenditure to encourage on savings. The development of all three sections is based on university students' environment in Malaysia. Usability testing is performed to evaluate the e-PF effectiveness, efficiency and satisfaction.

Methodology
In order to conduct the usability testing, bachelor degree students from Universiti Teknologi MARA (UiTM) Perlis Branch were selected randomly. In ensuring that the respondents come from different education background, students were selected from all seven different faculties in UiTM Perlis Branch. The respondents from each faculty were about four to ten students. Table 1 shows the classification of respondents.

Table 1: Classification of Respondents According to Field and Faculty

Field	Faculty
Science and Technology	Faculty of Applied Sciences Faculty of Computer and Mathematical Sciences Faculty of Architecture, Planning and Surveying Faculty of Sports Science and Recreation Faculty of Plantation and Agrotechnology
Business Management	Faculty of Accountancy Faculty of Business Management

Two types of usability methods were used in testing; questionnaires and expert review. The questionnaire and expert review questions were classified according to its measure and explanation as summarized in Table 2.

Table 2: Classification, Measure and Explanation of Usability Methods (Adapted from Current Practice in Measuring Usability (Hornbaek, 2006)

Classification	Measure	Explanation
Effectiveness	Experts' assessment Users' assessment	*Users' assessment of the outcomes of the interaction (quality of web system)*
Efficiency	Usage patterns	*Measures of how users make use of the interface to solve tasks*
Satisfaction	Perception of outcome	*Users' assessment of the outcomes of the interaction (assessment of own performance)*

Questionnaire questions regarding effectiveness measure users' assessment from their interaction with the quality of e-PF web system. Questions on efficiency measures users' usage patterns on how they make use of the interface to improve financial literacy and understand financial planning and management. As for satisfaction questions, users perception on the outcomes of their interaction with e-PF web system were gathered.

Expert review was used to only collect experts' assessment on the outcome of their interaction with the web system to analyze the effectiveness of e-PF as an education medium.

Results and Findings
A total of 50 students participated as questionnaire respondents. Respondents answered 18 questions to evaluate e-PF efficiency, effectiveness and users' satisfaction. The range response for each questionnaire question is between 1 (*Strongly Disagree*), 2 (*Somewhat Disagree*), 3 (*Neutral*), 4 (*Somewhat Agree*) and 5 (*Strongly Agree*). Table 3 tabulates the responses of the questionnaire.

Table 3: Responses to Questionnaire

No.	Efficiency	Mean Score
1	I know how to use e-PF.	3.94
2	The choice of words used is easy to understand.	3.88
3	Instructions for Financial Test, Budget Planner and Finance Calculator are clear and not confusing.	4.08
4	The questions in Financial Test are appropriate.	4.12
	Effectiveness	
5	The result that I got from Financial Test is acceptable.	4.04
6	My financial information that I put in Budget Planner is saved correctly and can be referred when needed.	4.20
7	Finance Calculator calculates accurately.	4.20
8	Finance Calculator calculates important financial activities for students.	4.24
9	All financial information in e-PF relate to students environment.	4.22
10	e-PF is effective to help students increase the understanding of personal finance.	4.32
	Satisfaction	
11	I am satisfy with financial information in all the sections (Financial Test, Budget Planner and Finance Calculator) in e-PF.	4.10
12	All the sections (Financial Test, Budget Planner and Finance Calculator) in e-PF are not complicated to use.	4.20
13	The sections (Financial Test, Budget Planner and Finance Calculator) are suitable for a new learner of personal finance.	4.14
14	The information in e-PF gives me new knowledge about personal finance.	4.16
15	e-PF helps me discover my behaviour in financial planning.	4.08
16	e-PF encourages me to change my attitude towards money management.	4.28
17	I am now more aware about my financial planning.	4.18
18	Besides using e-PF, I think personal finance subject should be taught to non-finance students.	4.28

The data collected shows that there were students *somewhat disagree* with the choice of words used in e-PF system because there were students who were not from Business Management field that were not familiar with some of the finance terminology. Consequently, that makes question 2 and question 3 responses slightly below mean score of 4. Nevertheless, from the overall questionnaire, it can determine that e-PF system is effective, efficient and fulfil users' satisfaction in helping them to increase financial literacy and thus improve their knowledge and attitude in financial planning and management. Interestingly, many of the students *strongly agree* that personal finance subject should be taught to non-finance students so that students from all fields and faculties can understand better about personal finance.

For the expert review, two finance lecturers participated to test the effectiveness of e-PF web system. Table 4 shows the expert review responses.

Table 4: Responses from Expert Review

Effectiveness – e-PF as an Education Medium	Mean
e-PF sections content (Financial Test, Budget Planner and Finance Calculator) are related with personal finance topic.	4.5
Questions in Financial Test are compatible with personal finance syllabus.	4.5
The result that I got from Financial Test is acceptable.	4.5
e-PF can be used as one of education medium to deliver financial literacy to students.	5.0

Both lecturers gave positive feedback towards the effectiveness of e-PF web system. One of the lecturer informed that e-PF is a good method for spreading about personal finance to university students. Another lecturer added that the combination of the three sections (Financial Test, Budget Planner and Finance Calculator) fulfils the personal finance requirements and specifications for students. As a result, both lecturers agree that e-PF can be used as one of the medium to deliver about personal finance to university students.

Conclusion and Future Works
The importance of personal finance literacy among university students becomes crucial because majority of the students are on education loan and have low money management skills. e-PF web system is developed to evaluate financial literacy of knowledge and attitude about personal finance among university students. Besides that, it functions to encourage financial planning and money management. These can be achieved through three sections consist of financial test, budget planner and finance calculator in e-PF web system.

From the findings, it can be concluded that using e-PF web system can help university students to improve their financial literacy towards better financial planning and money management. Many students agree that personal finance subject should be taught to all faculties. Significantly, expert reviews reach to an agreement that e-PF web system can be used as one of the education medium to provide financial literacy education to university students.

For future works, this web system can be improved by providing monthly and annually report summary on income, expenditure and savings. In addition, the report summary can be added with graphical presentation where students can visualize their integrated financial patterns. The web system functions can also be extended to include other areas of personal finance such as insurance and investment.

References
Bevan, N. (2009). Extending quality in use to provide a framework for usability measurement. *In International Conference on Human Centered Design*, Springer Berlin Heidelberg, pp. 13-22.

Chen, H. and Volpe, R.P. (1998). An Analysis of Personal Financial Literacy among College Students. *Financial Services Review*, 7(2), 107-128. Retrieved from
http://www.sciencedirect.com/science/article/pii/S1057081099800067

Cude, B. J., Lawrence F. L., Lyons, A.C., Metzger, K., LeJeune E., Marks L. and Machtmes K. (2006). College Students and Financial Literacy: What They Know and What We Need to Learn. *Eastern Family Economics and Resource Management Association 2006 Conference*, 102-109. Retrieved from

https://www.cgsnet.org/ckfinder/userfiles/files/College_Students_and_Fin
ancial_Literacy.pdf

Hornbaek, K. (2006) Current Practice in Measuring Usability: Challenges to
Usability Studies and Research. *International Journal of Human-
Computer Studies*, 64(2), 79-102. Retrieved from
http://www.sciencedirect.com/science/article/pii/S1071581905001138

Ibrahim, D., Harun, R., & Isa, Z. M. (2009). A Study on Financial Literacy of
Malaysian Degree Students. *Cross-Cultural Communication*, 5(4), 51–59.
Retrieved from
http://www.cscanada.net/index.php/ccc/article/viewFile/773/772

Jariah, M., Husniyah, A. R., Laily, P., & Britt, S. (2004). Financial Behavior
and Problems among University Students: Need for Financial Education.
Journal of Personal Finance, 3(1), 82–96. Retrieved from
http://childfinanceinternational.org/component/mtree/kb/global-
platforms/financial-education/financial-behavior-and-problems-among-
university-students-need-for-financial-education?Itemid=

Keown, A.J. (2010). Personal Finance: Turning Money into Wealth. Retrieved
from http://www.gbv.de/dms/zbw/799816930.pdf

Ahsan, M.H. (2013) Financial Literacy Research On Undergraduate Students
In Malaysia: Current Literature And Research Opportunities.
International Journal of Education and Research, 1(11). Retrieved from
http://www.ijern.com/journal/November-2013/35.pdf

OECD (2012). Financial Education: OECD PISA Financial Literacy
Assessment. Retrieved from
http://www.oecd.org/finance/financialeducation/oecdpisafinancialliteracya
ssessment.htm

Cameron, M. P., Calderwood, R., Cox, A., Lim, S., & Yamaoka, M. (2013).
Personal financial literacy among high school students in New Zealand,
Japan and the USA. Citizenship, *Social and Economics Education*, 12(3),
200-215.

Seddon, C. (2012). Measuring National Well-Being - Personal Finance. Office
of National Statistics. Retrieved from
http://webarchive.nationalarchives.gov.uk/20160105160709/http://www.o
ns.gov.uk/ons/dcp171766_278355.pdf

Toussaint-Comeau, M., and Rhine, S. L. W. (2000). Delivery of Financial
Literacy Programs. Retrieved from
http://citeseerx.ist.psu.edu/viewdoc/download?doi=10.1.1.196.6645&rep=
rep1&type=pdf

Article 10

Embedding Gamification Elements in Distributed Pair Programming (DPP): A Conceptual Framework

Mahfudzah Othman, Zulfikri Paidi, Noor Azilah Abu Bakar, Nurzaid Muhd Zain
Faculty of Computer & Mathematical Sciences
Universiti Teknologi MARA Perlis Branch

Abstract
This paper discusses a conceptual model of a web system for distributed pair programming (DPP) that involves the use of gamification elements as the new feature of the system. DPP is one of the efforts that support pair programming over geographically distributed environment. Pairs from dispersed locations can communicate with each other to code or completing tasks via the Internet. The proposed model involved the development of a web system that facilitates DPP with the use of web-based applications and web 2.0 tools. Nevertheless, in order to make the web system more fun and interactive, gamification elements are embedded in the proposed model. Suitable game mechanics based on gamification Octalysis Framework are selected that focused on the development and achievement of each pair in the DPP web system. The aim of the proposed model is not only to encourage the use of the gamified DPP web system but also to improve learners' experiences in learning programming that is stress free and more interactive.

Keywords: programming, distributed pair programming, gamification

Introduction

Pair programming has been widely implemented in the field of education with the aim to improve the quality of codes, boost the confidence of the students and making the process of learning more enjoyable (He & Chen, 2014).

Further discussion done by Nurzaid and Zulfikri (2015) has showed that pair programming can be a successful tool when implemented in programming classes. Among the positive impacts are students happened to be less frustrated with the outcomes from the pair programming sessions, becomes more trustworthy and developed more confident in their friendship. He and Chen (2014) also added that the creative process to produce many meaningful and quality codes had increased together with students' interests in learning programming with their partners.

Nonetheless, pair programming is mainly implemented in physical classrooms or computer laboratories where the interactions are visible and can be closely monitored by the lecturers. In the team effectiveness model proposed by Faja (2013) then discussed by Nurzaid and Zulfikri (2015), pair programming can also be employed in a virtual environment and it is called distributed pair programming (DPP). To implement DPP, it requires different academic settings and design, such as providing network access to the teams and lecturers from dispersed locations.

Furthermore, in order to make learning using DPP more enjoyable and engaging, gamification elements can be embedded into the features of the system. For instance, a study done by Li et al. (2013), has shown that gamifications when included in an e-learning platform, would encourage students to be more engaged and interested in the subject matter. In the study, they have used the PeerSpace, a collaborative learning environment with the support of Web 2.0 tools that promote student interactions on course-related topics as well as purely social matters. Among the gamification elements included in their system are the participation points, a level system based on participation points, a progress bar, leader boards, collaborative programming for community building and casual games (Li et al., 2013).

Therefore, the purpose of this paper is to discuss the proposed of a conceptual framework that describes the integration of gamification elements in a DPP environment. The aim is to provide a model or guideline of the development of a gamified e-learning system that supports DPP learning processes.

Background of Study
i. Pair Programming
Pair programming can be described as an agile software development technique that involves two programmers who are sitting on the same workstation and working on a same task together (Maguire et al., 2014). The task may involve designing and coding the same algorithm where each person plays

important role as the "driver" or "navigator" (Faja, 2013). During the pair programming session, the programmer who acts as the "driver" is taking charge on the mouse and keyboard while the other person who acts as the "navigator" observes the "driver" and offers suggestions and corrections to the algorithm or the codes (Faja, 2013; Li et al., 2013) . The roles as "driver" and "navigator" are interchangeable where each partner will be given chances to alternate their roles after certain period of time while collaborating in designing, coding and reviewing (Faja, 2013; Maguire et al., 2014). This technique is normally used to enhance software productivity at a higher level of software quality (Winkler et al., 2013).

ii. Team Effectiveness Model of Pair Programming
Team effectiveness model is to describe the main factors that will influence the success of the pair programming. The success of pair programming is contributed by the four factors in the team effectiveness model that has been discussed in recent study conducted by Faja (2013) as shown in Figure 1.

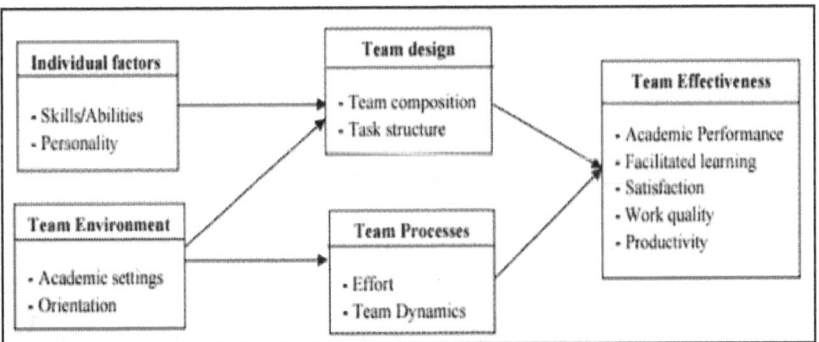

Figure 1: Team effectiveness model of pair programming

The first factor, which is the individual factor emphasizing on the importance of finding the right partner or pair based on the skills, abilities or personality (Faja, 2013). For instance, Chen and He (2014) claimed that for better performance, pairs should be assigned randomly, with disparity of academic performance. Other study suggested that matching pairs, with the same skill levels or academic performance would likely perform better and produce quality codes in a shorter amount of time (Zacharis, 2011), while some claimed that slight difference in pairs' skill levels will worked it best in pair programming (Kellaris & Backstrom, 2015).

The second factor is the team environment that emphasizes on the academic setting and orientation. The academic setting proposed in this model provides two different mechanisms, which are either practical session in traditional classrooms or implementation of pair programming in a virtual environment (Faja, 2011). While most of the previous studies focused on face-to-face interaction, other researchers have developed web applications to support the pair programming practice, especially in supporting distance learning. For instance, a web-based system named Online Collaborative Learning System (OCLS) has been developed to support pair collaboration and discussion for learning programming in a virtual environment. Although, the technique used in the study did not clearly mentioned the pair programming concept, however, the "Think-Pair-Share" technique embedded in the system has also reflected the adoption of pair programming approach (Mahfudzah, et al., 2013).

The third influential factor is the team design and task structure. The design of the team structure and task complexity has significant role in pair programming approach. Pair programming implementation involved set of rules and setting such as it needs to be implemented in a control in-class environment with only one workstation for each pair. Nonetheless, pair programming also can be implemented for outside assignments although this approach seemed to be difficult to control as students often found it difficult to collaborate due to conflicting schedules (Faja, 2011).

The final factor in the team effectiveness model is the team processes that involved team dynamics and effort. As mentioned by Braught and Wahls (2011), in ensuring positive pair interactions and efforts, lecturers or instructors must also be actively engaged in the whole pair programming process.

Switching roles between pairs has been suggested as one of the key elements that determine the dynamic of the pair. Having one person to constantly check the codes is another way to maintain the team dynamics and foster teamwork and communication skills (Kellaris & Backstrom, 2015).

iii. Distributed Pair Programming(DPP)

Pair programming is typically done as collocated activity with both programmers sharing control of a single physical computer, keyboard and mouse. Distributed pair programming (DPP) brings pair programming to the geographically distributed environment where collocated collaboration is not feasible. Furthermore, DPP is supported by technologies such as screen and desktop sharing as well as collaborative editors over the internet. In desktop sharing, all users, not only share a single screen, but also have simultaneous keyboard and mouse access (McKinsey, 2015). Teaching and learning can be more interesting and more efficient by using DPP instead of pair programming in the same location. As an example, the student and another student in the same group might be in the different locations, but can still connect with each other to complete the given tasks and formed their own virtual team. In general, a virtual team can be defined as a group of people who work together towards a common goal but operate across time, distance, culture and organizational boundaries (Bernado, 2012).

iv. Gamification in education

Gamification can be defined as the use of game mechanics in the non-game context such as in the field of education, health, financial and many others (Deterding et al., 2011). The aim of integrating gamification elements in learning is usually to contribute motivation principles and engagement based on the gaming concept into ordinary activities (Nah et al. 2013). Gamification in education can be seen as an alternative way to use game dynamics and game mechanics in the scope of learning with the aim to motivate students to become more engaged in the process of learning and interacting with other students (Lee et al, 2011).

v. Gamifications in e-Learning

Developing and deploying effective e-learning programs can give many advantages in teaching and learning process. According to Nagarajan et al. (2010), one of the advantages in using e-learning is that it is more cost effective where it promotes paperless environment, no delays, no physical classrooms are needed and does not involve travel expenses. It also enables tutor and learner to take what they have just learned from their computer screens and apply it to the task at hand (Nagarajan et al., 2010).

Gamification in e-learning platforms also can make the process of learning and teaching becomes more interactive and effective. According to Deterding et al., (2011), gamification, however, offers a whole new set of opportunities to make the students more involved, such as clear goals with variety of ways to approach them, curiosity, and systems of challenges, constraints and achievements.

Meanwhile, gamification also offers the concept of accomplishment, which refers to an impressive thing that is done or achieved after a lot of work. Students can earn badges by completing certain tasks, solving certain exercise first, attaining certain levels in specific amount of time, achieving success in challenges, contest and being active on the forum (Swacha et al., 2013). By doing this, students can feel that challenges in study are more important and powerful and can trigger them to emphasize their learning.

Proposed of Conceptual Framework of the Gamified Distributed Pair Programming (DPP)

As depicted in Figure 2, the proposed conceptual model consists of combinations of few different elements. The first element is the pair programming technique that was adapted from the team effectiveness model discussed by Faja (2013). As the development of DPP is aimed to cater pairs that located in different locations, therefore lecturers need to consider the individual factors to form the pairings. In this case, we proposed the difference between students' programming skills as the pairing motive. The idea was to encourage the low achievers to learn and perform better when partnered with their high achiever friends.

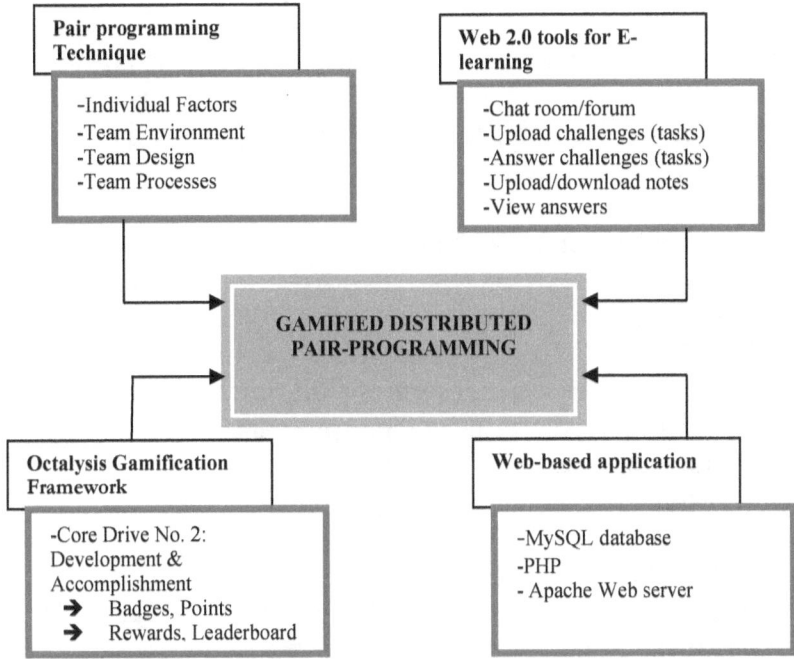

Figure 2: A conceptual model of gamified distributed pair-programming

The next factor is pivotal, which involves academic setting an orientation. Since DPP is a pair programming implemented in a virtual environment, the orientation of the pairs depends on their identifications or tags to ensure the role as driver and navigator can be interchangeable. For this purpose, we proposed the use of gamification elements in the system such as avatar or emoji to identify the virtual teams. Meanwhile, to ensure the effectiveness of DPP or virtual pair programming, the development of the online system involved the web-based application tools such as the MySQL database, PHP and Apache web server.

The third factor according to the team effectiveness model is the team design that includes the construction of tasks. In this model, the selected topics for the tasks were taken from the introductory programming course and the questions constructed were based on the six levels of the Bloom's Taxonomy cognitive domains comprising of Knowledge, Comprehension, Application, Analysis, Synthesis and Evaluation. The objective is to encourage the students or pairs to answer questions from the easiest level, which is Knowledge and progressing until they reach the hardest level, which is Evaluation.

The final factor involves the team processes. The development of this system must ensure to retain the dynamics of the pairs and interactions between students and lecturers. We proposed the use of Web 2.0 tools to support teams' communication and collaboration. Meanwhile, to ensure the interactivity and fun learning while answering the programming questions, gamification elements were also proposed to be embedded in the system's assessment modules.

The gamification elements selected for this system consist of suitable game mechanics and game dynamics that support DPP functionalities as well acting as catalyst to improve learners' engagements. In order to select the suitable gamification elements for this project, the Octalysis Framework developed by Chao (2015) was referred. This gamification framework consists of eight core drives, which are Development and Accomplishment, Epic Meaning and Calling, Empowerment of Creativity and Feedback, Social Influence and Relatedness, Unpredictability and Curiosity, Loss and Avoidance, Scarcity and Impatience and Ownership and Possession. Each of the core drive has different meanings and aims. For instance, if the system focusing on Development and Accomplishment, few game mechanics are proposed to use such as points, rewards, progress bar, ranking, leader board, step-by-step tutorial and many others Chao (2015).

Other core drives involved the use of narrative, elitism, humanity hero for Epic Meaning and Calling, social invitations, social treasures, group quest and mentorship for Social Influence and Relatedness and the use of visual storytelling, mini quests and random rewards for Unpredictability and Curiosity. Meanwhile, the gamified system can also focus on using the core drive Loss and Avoidance by using game mechanics such as sunk-cost tragedy, progress loss and scarlet letter or using countdown, throttles, patient feedback, appointment dynamics for Scarcity and Impatience and finally using virtual goods, built from scratch, avatar, collection sets, recruitment and monitoring for Ownership and Possession (Chao, 2015). Any gamified systems can have one or combinations of these core drives and can be applied in either the assessment module, social interactions or tasks.

For the purpose of this project, we proposed only one core drive based on the Octalysis Framework, which is the Development and Accomplishment". This core drive focuses on using game mechanics such as badges, points, rewards and leader board and often relates to learning progression, practicing, competition, collaboration, tutoring, and eventually overcoming challenges (Chao, 2015). The word "challenge" here means giving something such as badge or trophy or appreciation in order to make the challenges becomes more meaningful (Chao, 2015).

Based on the proposed conceptual model, we had developed the DPP web system. Via the system, the pairs were given set of tasks by the lecturers. The tasks needed to be completed within teams consist of different levels of difficulties as mentioned in the previous section. Each pair needed to unlock each level of question and were given points, rewards and badges for all correct answers. Finally, at the end of each session of the online tasks, the leader board displayed the ranks of the teams based on the points collected by each pair. This concept will encourage the team to collaborate, compete with each other and score in each task.

Conclusion

In conclusion, the proposed conceptual model of gamified distributed pair programming (DPP) is seen as an effort to support the practices of distributed pair programming where coders or students can discuss and collaborate to produce better codes over the Internet. Moreover, in order to make the learning process and experience more enjoyable, the gamification elements were integrated into the web system. Among the game mechanics proposed embedded into the system are badges, extra points and giving out rewards to the pairs that successfully completed the given tasks and produce error-free codes. It is expected that by introducing the game mechanics in the learning process, students or programmers will become dynamic coders and more confident in producing better codes, thus helping them to improve their performances in programming courses as well.

References

Bernardo Jose da Silva Est'cio. (2012). Development of a Set of Best Practices for Distributed Pair Programming. *IEEE Seventh International Conference on Global Software Engineering Workshops*, pp. 33 – 34.

Braught, G., & Wahls, T. (2011). The Case for Pair Programming in the Computer science Classroom, *ACM Transactions on Computing Education*, 11(1). New York, NY, US.

Chao, Y, K. (2015). *Actionable Gamification: Beyond Points, Badges, and Leaderboard*, USA: Octalysis Media.

Deterding. S., Dixon, D., Khaled, R. & Nacke, L. (2011). From Game Design Elements to Gamefulness: Defining Gamification. *Proceedings of MindTrek*, pp. 9-15.

Faja, S. (2011). Pair programming as a team based learning activity: A review of research, *Issues in Information Systems*, Vol XII, No. 2, pp. 207-216.

Faja, S. (2013). Evaluating Effectiveness of Pair Programming as a Teaching Tool in Programming Courses, *Proc. Information Systems Educators Conference*, pp. 1-10.

He, X & Chen, Y. (2014). *Analyzing the Efficiency of Pair Programming in Education*. Bachelor of Science Thesis, University of Gothenburg.

Kellaris, I. & Backstrom, P. (2015). *Effects of Personality and Expertise on Pair Programming A comprehensive literature review on the effects of personality and expertise on pair programming, with the purpose to lay a foundation for how to configure pairs*, Bachelor of Science Thesis, University of Gothenburg.

Lee, J. J. & Hammer, J. (2011). Gamification in Education: What, How, Why Bother? *Academic Exchange Quarterly*, 15(2).

Li,C., Dong, Z., Untch, R.H & Chasteen, M. (2013). Engaging Computer Science Students through Gamification in an Online Social Network Based Collaborative Learning Environment, *Int. Journal of Information and Education Technology*, Vol. 3, No. 1, pp.72 - 77.

Mahfudzah, O., Muhaini, O., & Fazlin Marini, H. (2013). Designing Prototype Model of an Online Collaborative Learning System for Introductory Computer Programming Course, *Procedia - Social and Behavioral Sciences 90*, pp. 293 – 302.

Maguire, P., Maguire, R., Hyland, P. & Marshall, P. (2014). Enhancing Collaborative Learning Using Pair Programming: Who Benefits? *All Ireland Journal in Teaching and Learning in Higher Education* (AISHE – J), Vol. 6, Number 2, pp. 1411-14124.

McKinsey, J. (2015). Remote Pair Programming in a Visual Programming Language. Technical Report. *Electrical Engineering and Computer Sciences*, University of California, pp.1-37.

Nagarajan, P., & Wiselin Jijil, G. (2010). Online Education System (E-Learning). *International Journal of Online Service, Science and Technology*, 3(4), pp.37- 48.

Nah, F.F., Telaprolu, V.R. & Rallapali, S. (2013). Gamification of education using computer games background, *Gamification and Its Application to Education*, pp. 99-107.

Nurzaid, M.Z. & Zulfikri, P. (2015). Pair Programming: An Overview. *Proc. in Colloquium in Computer and Mathematical Science Education* (CCMSE 2015), pp. 7-11.

Swacha, J., & Baszuro, P. (2015). Gamification Based on E-learning Platform for Computer Programming Education. *Conference on Computer in Education*, pp.123-130.

Winkler, D., Kitzler, M., Steindl, C. & Biffl, S. (2013). Investigating the impact of experience and solo/pair programming on coding efficiency: Results and experiences from coding contests, *In: H. Baumeister and B. Weber (Eds.), Agile Processes in Software Engineering and Extreme Programming, LNBIP*, Vol. 149, Springer-Verlag Berlin Heidelberg, 2013, pp.106-120.

Zacharis, N. Z. (2011). Measuring the Effects of Virtual Pair Programming in an Introductory Programming Java Course, *IEEE Transactions on Education*, 54(1), pp. 168-170.

Article 11

Construction of Mobile Fidyah Calculator

Arifah Fasha Rosmani
Faculty of Computer & Mathematical Sciences
Universiti Teknologi MARA Perlis Branch

Asiah Ismail, Noor Azura Kamarudin
Academy of Contemporary Islamic Studies
Universiti Teknologi MARA Perlis Branch

Abstract

Fidyah is the fine for Muslims who are not able to qada (replace) their fast during the current Ramadhan month until the next Ramadhan. Fidyah can be paid in cash or in the form of food such as rice or dates, and it can only be given to poor Muslims who are permitted to accept Zakat. Mobile Fidyah Calculator is designed and developed for Muslims to get accurate calculation of Fidyah. Mobile Fidyah Calculator provides the calculation of rice in Kilogram (kg) as a person should pay Fidyah according to the type of rice they consumed. Mobile Fidyah Calculator also provides a guidance and information that help the users to increase their knowledge about Fidyah.

Keywords: *Fidyah, mobile, android, qada, fasting.*

Introduction

Fidyah is an obligatory practice in Islam for Muslims in certain cases (Ahmad, 2010). Fidyah is the compensation that needs to be paid for the fasting days, which could not be performed due to several reasons such as having a chronic illness or being on a journey (musafir).

"[Fasting for] a limited number of days. So whoever among you is ill or on a journey [during them] - then an equal number of days [are to be made up]. And upon those who are able [to fast, but with hardship] - a ransom [as substitute] of feeding a poor person [each day]. And whoever volunteers excess - it is better for him. But to fast is best for you, if you only knew." (Surah Al-Baqarah:184)

It can also be described as a penalty for not fasting during the Ramadan month until the next Ramadan, due to accepted reasons or delay in replacing fasting days (Possumah & Ismail, 2012). Those who are permitted to be excused from fasting can compensate by giving alms to the poor (Gilani, 2011). The amount of Fidyah that are to be distributed to the poor is based on a specified weight of particular food commodities such as crops like rice (the staple food of the population). Fidyah calculation varies according to the price of rice set by the government (Majlis Agama Islam Wilayah Persekutuan, 2016).

Nowadays, Muslims are not aware about Fidyah; they do not know how to calculate and how to pay for it in a proper way. If this issue continues, there will be no awareness in each Muslim on the importance of Fidyah and they will not consider it as their obligation. To prevent this, there is a need to develop an application that will assist and guide them in completing one of the most important responsibilities as Muslims.

Thus, this project aims to develop a mobile application, which can calculate the accurate calculation of Fidyah for Muslims. It is designed to ease the process of Fidyah calculation based on type of rice consumed in Kilogram (kg).

Related Works
There are two existing website systems in the market, which are Kalkulator Fidyah (secure.zakatsel.com.my) and Kalkulator Fidyah (E-muamalat). Both are web-based applications, which are used to calculate Fidyah. It is almost similar to Mobile Fidyah Calculator except that when compared to the existing calculators' technique, this application proposes a new paradigm in calculating Fidyah as it uses a mobile platform. This mobile application also focuses on the aspects of usability, interface design and functionality.

i. Kalkulator Fidyah
Kalkulator Fidyah (secure.zakatsel.com.my) has been developed by Zakat Selangor (Figure 1). This website calculates the amount of Fidyah based on the data entered by users. The users need to key in their details such as name, IC number and address. Users

are required to fill up just simple data; the calculation is also easy to understand. Although, the interface is very simple with plain background, unfortunately, this page can no longer be accessed due to excessive traffic conditions.

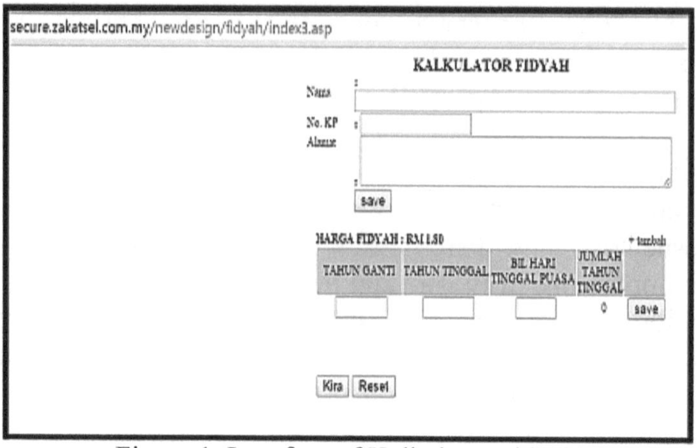

Figure 1: Interface of Kalkulator Fidyah

ii. e-Muamalat: Kalkulator Fidyah

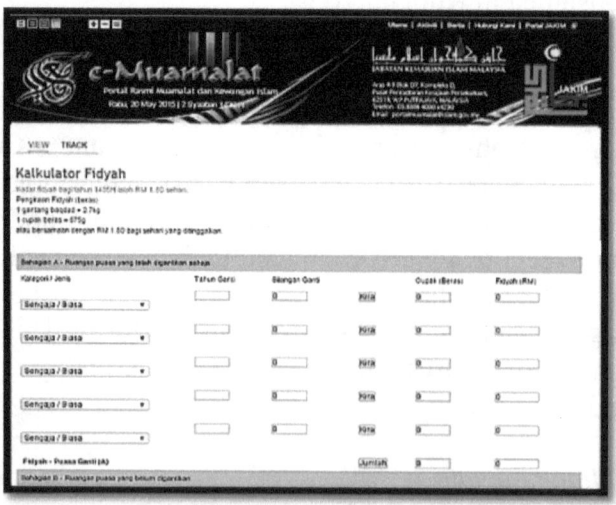

Figure 2: Interface of e-Muamalat: Kalkulator Fidyah

e-Muamalat: Kalkulator Fidyah (*e-muamalat.islam.gov.my/kalkulator-fidyah*) website is designed to calculate Fidyah for Muslims who have delayed the fasting days due to a particular excuse. "E-muamalat" website is handled by Jabatan Kemajuan Islam Malaysia (JAKIM). The design of the interface is interesting and it also provides an explanation about Fidyah. However, there are too many text fields that users need to fill up and this might confuse them.

Methodology
In this research, a new model has been mapped based on a Waterfall Model; it uses a sequential design process, in which progress is seen as flowing steadily downwards and is frequently used in software development processes (Balaji &Murugaiyan, 2010). The requirement for every phase should be clear in the process of developing Mobile Fidyah Calculator. Below are the processes involved in the project:

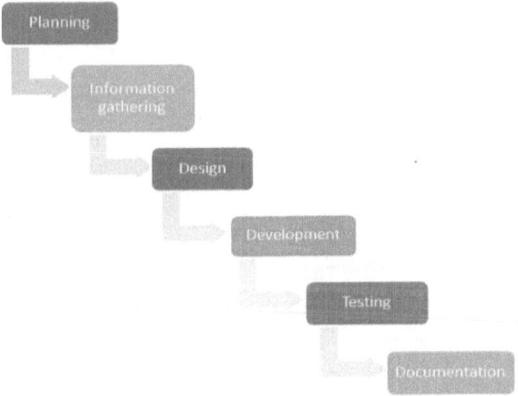

Figure 3: Methodology

i.   Planning: Finding information about Fidyah and study all the requirements needed in the project.
ii.   Information gathering: Searching for all the information that are related to the topic and understand the users' requirements.
iii. Designing: Creating a sitemap and a wireframe to design the interface of Mobile Fidyah Calculator.
iv.   Developing: Write a Java script and combine the entire interface.

v.   Testing: Test users' satisfaction levels after they have used the application.

vi. Documenting: Document all the activities as a final report.

i. Design and Development
This paper will focus only on the design and development phase.

a) Sitemap Design
A sitemap is a visual or a textually organized model of an application content that allows users to navigate through the application to find the information that they are searching for. A sitemap is designed before the development process. From the sitemap, the developer gets an idea on how to design the interface and the whole function of the application. The sitemap tells users how the application works and this makes it easier for users to use the application because each page listed in a sitemap is typically linked to the page it represents. This allows visitors to quickly jump to any section of an application listed in the sitemap.

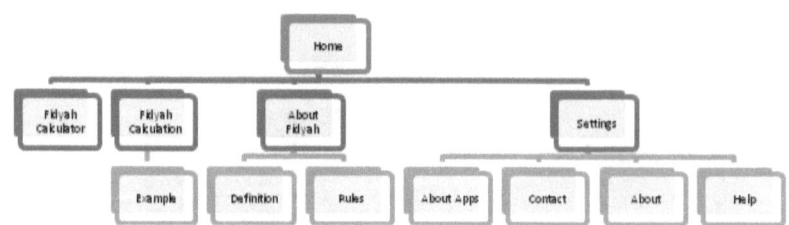

Figure 4: Sitemap

Figure 4 shows the design of the sitemap of Mobile Fidyah Calculator. The sitemap was designed to construct the flow of the application. It is organized hierarchically, breaking down the application information into specific subject areas. The first pageis the Home page, which includes three main menu buttons which are "About Fidyah", "Fidyah Calculation" and "Fidyah Calculator". Meanwhile, action bar contains "About Apps", "Contact", "About" and "Help". This application is focused on

Fidyah Calculator, which calculates the amount of the Fidyah according to the data entered by users.

b) Wireframe Design

A wireframe, which is also known as screen blueprint or page schematic, represents the framework of a website or an application. Wireframe describes the page layout. It is a series of drawings or designs that shows the arrangement sequence of every page. Before developing the project, the developer will design the interface of an application using suitable software, and for Mobile Fidyah Calculator, Balsamiq Mockups is used to design the interface. The drawing is not too fancy, just a simple basic shapes, stick figures and simple backgrounds. This is to construct an idea before developing an actual application. Designing the wireframe helps the developer to plan how to develop the real application and the developer can make changes on the wireframe, if he/she changes his/ her mind later. Figure 5 shows the design of the wireframe of Fidyah Calculator application.

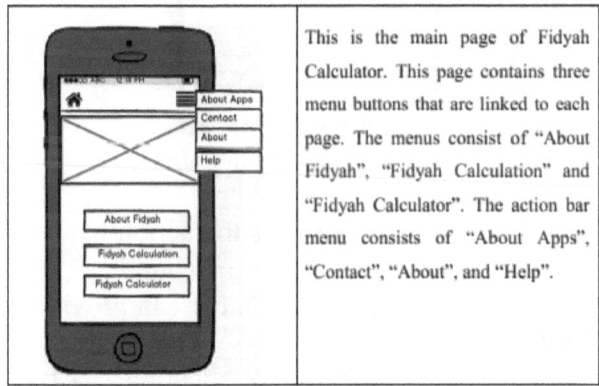

Figure 5: Example of a wireframe design

c) Interface Design

Home page is the main menu interface for Fidyah Calculator Application. This page has three menu buttons which are "About Fidyah", "Fidyah Calculation" and "Fidyah Calculator". These three buttons are represented together with images. Meanwhile, the action bar consists of four menus, "About Apps", "Contact", "About" and "Help", which are included with icons.

This is Fidyah Calculator, which is to calculate the Fidyah amount based on the data entered by users. Users need to enter the year they have replaced fast, the year they have missed fast and the number of days missed. When they click the calculate button, it will compute the result and display it on the text field. Reset button function is to clear all the data in the text box. Figure 6 shows the example of the main interface of Fidyah Calculator Application.

Figure: 6: main interface

The app bar, which is also known as the action bar, is one of the most important design elements in building an Android application. This is because the action bar can provide interactive elements that are familiar to users. This Fidyah Calculator provides information about the application. "About Apps", "Contact", "About" and "Help" can assist users to understand the application. These action bars use a combination of words and icons. Figure 7 shows the action bar interface of Fidyah Calculator.

Figure 7: action bar interface

Fidyah Calculator is a page used to calculate the amount of Fidyah based on the data entered by users. There are three user inputs that users need to fill up. The first text field is "YEAR REPLACED FAST", which is the year users replaced fast, "YEAR MISSED FAST" is the year users missed fast, and "NO. OF FASTING DAY MISSED" is the number of days users missed fast. When they click the "CALCULATE" button, it will compute the amount of Fidyah in Kilogram (kg), while the "RESET" button is to reset all the data in the text fields. "CONVERT" button will pop up a message that explains how to convert the amount that they get in Kilogram into Ringgit Malaysia (RM). Figure 4.4 shows the examples of data entered by users to calculate the amount of Fidyah in Kilogram (kg).

Example:
Siti has missed3 fasting days in 2009, and she replaced the missed days in 2015. The calculation will be:
2015 – 2009 = 6years - (1 year) = 5years
5years x 3days x 0.68kg = 10.20 kg

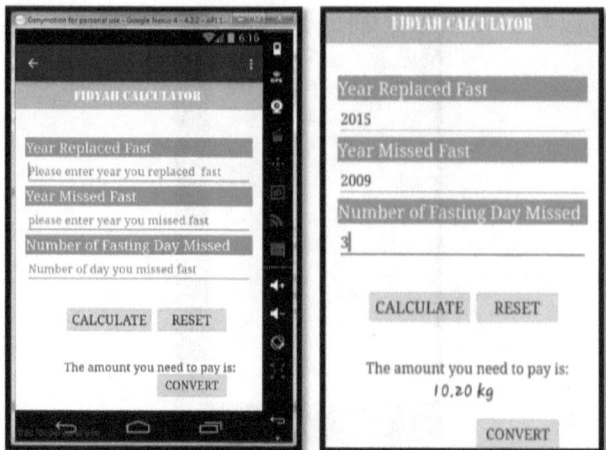

Figure 8: Fidyah calculator

Results and Analysis

There are three types of testing that have beenconducted;1) User Acceptance Test, 2) Usability Test, and 3) Heuristic Evaluation. User Acceptance Test and Usability Test were carried out to get the respond and to collect data from respondents about Fidyah Calculator. There were 30 respondents who were students and lecturers from non-IT background. Heuristic Evaluation was conducted by lecturers from Computer Science Department, Universiti Teknologi MARA (UiTM) Perlis Branch who are considered as experts in application development. This paper will only discuss User Acceptance Test result and analysis.

i.   User Acceptance Test

User Acceptance Test (UAT) is the test done when the system is completed and will be tested by the real-world audience. The purpose of this test is to find out whether the users can accept the application or not and to know whether this application is useful or not. The test was done by 30 respondents including students and people around UiTM Perlis Branch. The participants were given a mobile phone to use and navigate through Mobile Fidyah Calculator application, and then they were asked to answer a questionnaire. Table 1 shows the measurement criteria used in questionnaire for acceptance test:

Table 1: Measurement Criteria

Rank	Value
Strongly Agree	5
Agree	4
Not Sure	3
Disagree	2
Strongly Disagree	1

The measurement criteria have a ranking from 1 to 5, where 5 values the highest with strongly agree and 1 values the lowest with strongly disagree.

ii. User Acceptance Test Result

The result obtained from the evaluation of user acceptance test was gathered, analysed, and can be viewed in table below. Table 2 shows the mean score gathered from user acceptance test. The values of mean were calculated to get the average from the result obtained.

Respondents were provided with six evaluation questions after they had used the application. For question 1, 60% of the respondents strongly agreed that they could understand the definition of Fidyah. While, 40% of them strongly agreed that they could understand the example of Fidyah calculation.

For question 3, 57% of respondents were able to fill-in the data in the text field to calculate the Fidyah amount. Some of them faced a problem while trying to fill-in the data, this might be caused by the terms used in the application. Some of them did not understand what value they should enter in text field. To overcome this problem, this mobile application should change and use more suitable terms for Fidyah calculator page.

Table 2: Mean Score for User Acceptance Test

No	Description	1	2	3	4	5	Mean
1	I can understand the definition of Fidyah.	-	-	-	12	18	4.6
2	I can understand the example of Fidyah calculation.	-	-	-	18	12	4.4
3	I am able to fill-in the data in text field.	-	-	1	12	17	4.5
4	This application helps me gain knowledge about Fidyah.	-	-	-	2	28	4.9
5	This application helps me to calculate the amount of Fidyah rather than using manual calculation.	-	-	-	2	28	4.9
6	This application is useful.	-	-	-	1	29	4.97

Other than that, for question 4 and 5, 93% strongly agreed that this mobile application helped them gain more knowledge about Fidyah and calculate the amount of Fidyah more easily rather than using the manual calculation. Meanwhile, for question 6, 97% of the respondents strongly agreed that this application is useful. In a conclusion, the objectives for this application design have been achieved since most of the respondents gave a good response and it was found usable by them.

Conclusion and Future Works

There are several benefits of Mobile Fidyah Calculator, one of them is, users are able to get information about Fidyah. Fidyah Calculator is also usable and easy to use even for first time users, because it only provides three menu buttons on the main interface page. They just need to click the menu they want, and it will go the next page. The interface is also attractive and interesting because it is not crowded and does not include unrelated information.

The use of the background colour is also suitable and encourages users to use the application. Fidyah Calculator helps Muslims to calculate and get the accurate amount of Fidyah in a mobile environment rather than using manual calculation. It also adapts the concept of Multimedia Learning Principles to make the application attractive and usable to the users. These principles are applied by combining images together with words, to assist the users to understand better.

There are few recommendations that can be done for Fidyah Calculator's improvement. All the recommendations can be analysed from the comments and suggestions from the respondents from User Acceptance Test, Usability Test, and Heuristic Test. Currently, this application provides information about Fidyah, how the calculation is done and how to calculate the Fidyah in Kilogram (kg) only. In the users' test, a few respondents suggested that the application should be able to convert the amount of Fidyah into Ringgit Malaysia (RM).

Besides that, the application can be enhanced by adding another language, such as Malay language or Arabic language; it is because some users might not understand the information given in English. Other information about Fidyah can also be added, such as how to pay Fidyah and where they can pay it.

As a conclusion, we can conclude that the project has achieved the objectives. Fidyah Calculator is useful to the users because it can help Muslims to get information and calculate the amount of Fidyah. This is an alternative way to get the accurate amount rather than using manual calculation. This application also provides the calculation in Kilogram (kg) because a person can pay the Fidyah according to the type of rice they eat.

References

Ahmad, R. (2010). *Amalan Fidyah dalam masyarakat Islam di Kanchong Darat, Banting, Selangor: satu analisis/Rumaizi bin Ahmad* Doctoral dissertation, University of Malaya.

Balaji, S., &Murugaiyan, M. S. (2012). Waterfall vs. V-Model vs. Agile: A comparative study on SDLC. *International Journal of Information Technology and Business Management, 2*(1), 26-30.

Gilani, A., Davies, M., &Khunti, K. (2014). Religious fasting, Ramadan and hypoglycemia in people with diabetes. *Diabetic Hypoglycemia*, 7(1), 15-19.

Possumah, B.T., & Ismail, A. G. (2012). Baitul Mal and Legal Constraint: Public Wealth Management in Malaysian Context. *International Journal of Academic Research in Business and Social Sciences*, 2(11), 27-52.

Majlis Agama Islam Wilayah Persekutuan. (2016). *Fidyah*. Retrieved from http://www.maiwp.gov.my/i/index.php/perkhidmatan-kami/fidyah

Article 12

Developing a Personal Recommender System for Homestay Services using TOPSIS Method

Azmi Abu Seman, Norfiza Ibrahim, Sarah Zaffan Ruhani
Faculty of Computer & Mathematical Sciences
Universiti Teknologi MARA Perlis Branch

Abstract

Homestay Perlis recommender system is a web-based application system developed for users to find the best homestay services in Perlis. This system functions as: i) recommending the best homestay in Perlis and ii) receive review of homestays from the users. User requirements were identified through a survey. A set of questionnaire was distributed, and several criteria to select a homestay were identified. The collected data from experienced users were used to calculate the result using TOPSIS method. From the requirements, an application of a recommender system was designed and developed. The advantage of this system is the recommendations for the homestay are based on the criteria that meet users' priority. Besides that, the system able to help users to make a right decision in order to choose a homestay that meets their preferences and requirements. The usability test and the user acceptance test were conducted in the study. Results from usability test that focuses on the system's design, navigation, content, understanding and interactivity show that the recommender system is easy to navigate, fast loading and easy to understand. The user acceptance test measures the aspects of developing a website which are reactions to the website, interface design, navigation and the content for developing a website, which indicates high mean values showing that the recommender system is accepted by the users. Generally, the objectives of this research are successfully achieved.

Keywords: homestay services, recommender system, tourism, user satisfaction, web-based system

Introduction

Accommodation is a vital aspect of the tourism product towards the tourists. The style, degree and landscape of accommodation define the capacity and worth of tourism that is potential at any destination. Tourist accommodation typically refers to traditional hotels of several categories, while alternative accommodation refers to establishments such as Guest houses, Service apartments and Commercial homes that provide paid to the tourists on short-term basis (Gunasekaran.N & Anandkumarb, 2012). Homestay is one of the alternative accommodations that are provided for the tourists with an authentic and local touch.

Due to the issue, the study focuses on the method of selecting the best homestay services based on fuzzy logic approach. A recommender system will be developed by using the method in order to help users to choose a homestay based on their preferences. Users will choose their favourites based on the criteria provided; therefore, the system will generate a result and suggest the best homestay service that meets their need. This recommender system will become a new medium to recommend and provide the information to people who want to make a decision on selecting the best homestay services.

TOPSIS Method
i. Introduction
Multi Criteria Decision Making (MCDM) model based on fuzzy set theory refers to making decisions in the presence of multiple, usually conflicting, criteria. This relates to the selection of homestay that satisfies all the required criteria. There are several methods in MCDM, however, Technique for Order of Preference by Similarity to Ideal Solution (TOPSIS) method has been chosen in this study. The principle of the TOPSIS method is that the chosen alternatives should have the shortest distance from the ideal solution to the negative ideal solution.

ii. TOPSIS
TOPSIS method was first developed by Hwang and Yoon is one of the methods used to solve MCDM. The most crucial principle in TOPSIS is that the chosen alternatives should have the longest distance from the negative ideal solution and the shortest distance from the positive-ideal solution (Hwang and Yoon, 1981). This method is selected because it has simple process and also easy to program. Apart from that, the method is easy to understand and have the capability to remain the same quantity of the steps although there is problem about the size. However, TOPSIS

method has its disadvantages. The Euclidean distance does not look at connection of attributes besides it is hard to weight and retain stability of judgement (Velasques& Hester, 2013).

In addition, in traditional TOPSIS, the rating and weight of the criteria are known precisely. However, there are many real situations involved crisp data, which are inadequate to represent the real life situation due to vagueness of human judgements and cannot be estimated with precise numeric values (Hwang and Yoon, 1981). In order to resolve the vagueness that often arising in information from human judgements, fuzzy set theory has been integrated in many MCDM methods including TOPSIS.

According to Ahi, Aryanezhad, Ashtiani and Makui (2009), TOPSIS method consists of a few steps that are explained in the Research Method. In fuzzy TOPSIS, all the ratings and weights are defined by means of linguistic variables. A linguistic variable is defined as variable which values are sentences in a natural or artificial language (Zadeh, 1973) and linguistically, useful and beneficial (Zimmermann, 1991) in dealing with the situation due to the concept of linguistic variable that is very difficult to be explained as a pre-set amount of terms.

Research Method
There are four phases involved in the study; i) Planning, ii) Design, iii) Implementation, and iv) Testing.

i. Phase 1: Planning
The area of the study has been defined during the feasibility study. In this study, web-based application was chosen as a recommender system for selecting the homestay services in Perlis. Besides, the study aims to identify the best homestay service using a web-based recommender based on MCDM approach using TOPSIS method.The web-based recommender became assistance that recommends homestay based on users' preferences. Hence, the time taken for the users to select the best homestay service can be reduced.

Apart from that, all the information that related with this study was gathered and few journals and articles were reviewed together with the theoretical study on fuzzy logic, homestay services, MCDM and TOPSIS method. The deliverable in this phase is the literature review.

Other study that was conducted in this phase is finding the homestays that were included in this study. Homestays that available in Perlis according to the official directory of Ministry-registered homestays are Homestay Kampung Ujung Bukit, Homestay PayaGuring and Homestay Felda Mata Ayer. The criteria that influenced the selection of the homestays also were studied by distributing a set of questionnaire to 30 respondents. They were asked to select 7 criteria from 15 in the list of the questionnaire to find the most preferred criteria when choosing a homestay. The outcome from this activity is the 7 most chosen criteria by the respondents which are; price, safety, location, facility, comfortable, Internet service, and cleanliness.

Figure 1 display the overall phases with activities and outcomes of the study and the descriptions of each phase are described in the following sub-sections.

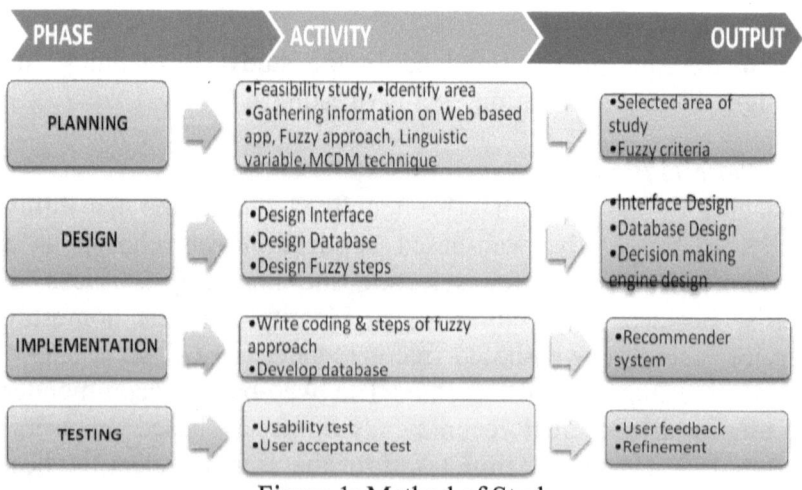

Figure 1: Method of Study

ii. Phase 2: Design
The activities that involved in this phase were designing the interface and the contents of the website. Besides that, designing a database and the steps in the TOPSIS method were included in this phase. The interface of a website played an important role to attract the users to return back once they had visit the website. Hence, the interfaces of the website have been designed by using Axure RP Pro 7.0. The second activity involved was designing a database. phpMyAdmin has been used as a tool to design the database in order to come out with the database design structure.
Next activity is designing the recommender system using TOPSIS method. There are few steps involved (Ahi, Aryanezhad, Ashtiani and Makui, 2009) which are:

Step 1: Calculate normalized decision matrix.
Step 2: Calculate weighted normalized decision matrix.
Step 3: Define positive ideal solution and negative ideal solution.
Step 4: Compute the distances of each of the alternatives from positive ideal solution and negative ideal solution using equations.
Step 5: Calculate the relative closeness to the ideal solution.
Step 6: Rank order of priority.

iii. Phase 3: Implementation
In this phase, Adobe Dreamweaver is used to write the coding using PHP language, phpMyAdminfor the database which provides the recommender system.

iv. Phase 4: Testing
There were two testing that were conducted in this phase, which are usability test and user acceptance test. In the usability test, the user was assigned to complete the tasks given. During the test, the user was observed and the feedbacks on functionality are taken for refinement. User acceptance was carried out to investigate the user feedbacks toward the system. A set of questionnaire has been distributed to the users and they were

asked whether the system able to meet their expectation. The result from the questionnaire has been documented as a research finding.

Findings and Analysis
i.   Usability Testing
Usability testing is one of the techniques to ensure that the users that are using the system are able to carry out the assigned tasks effectively, efficiently and satisfactorily (Gaffney, 1999). Each of the respondents is given their time to provide feedbacks on the tested system. For this study, there is 10 respondents from various backgrounds were chosen to perform the tasks.

a)   Website of Homestay Perlis Users
The respondents need to complete all of the ten tasks provided. They were interacted with the system based on the design, navigation, content, understanding and interactivity and give their comments and suggestions during the testing for improvement purposes.

Based on the observation, all of the tasks that were assigned to the respondents were successfully accomplished. They could understand the instructions stated in the website without any guideline given from the researcher. However, there were some parts of the website that need to be improved in order to make the website more user-friendly. The details of the refinements are explained in the next sub-section.

b)   Refinement of the Website
Based on the observation and feedback from the respondents, the recommender system were refined to ensure that the website met the users' need satisfied them. The refinement details were explained in following Table 1 and Table 2.

Table 1: Change the Feedback Response of the Result for Homestay Review

Before Refinement	After Refinement
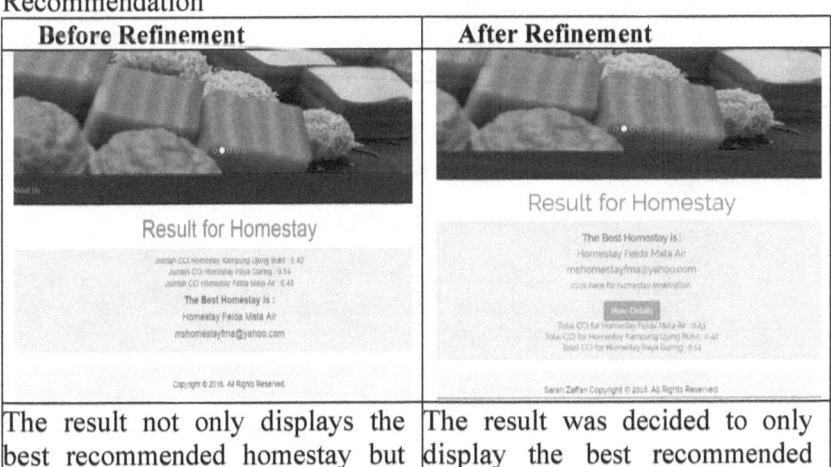	
The feedback response was quite simple. Besides, the users felt that it was quite difficult to proceed with the Homestay Recommendation since they need to return back to the Main Page and made the choice all over again.	The continue button was added to ease the users to proceed with the Homestay Recommendation. Besides, if they choose to not continue, they will simply returned back to the Main Page.

Table 2: Change the Pattern of the Result for Homestay Recommendation

Before Refinement	After Refinement
The result not only displays the best recommended homestay but also displays the result of the other homestays with their total Cci. The interface looked quite	The result was decided to only display the best recommended homestay. However, if the users want to view the details of the result, they can simply hit the

cluttered at the first impression. Besides, the homestays were not ranked according to their total Cci.	More Details button. The new interface of this page is more organized compared to the previous version.

From the analysis, it can be concluded that the users of the website of Homestay Perlis could complete the tasks given successfully. The recommender system is easy to navigate, fast loading and easy to understand.

ii. User Acceptance Test

After the refinement of the website is done, a user acceptance test was conducted in order to find out the user acceptance. The users were given a questionnaire and were asked to answer all questions based on their observation and perception on the recommender system. There are 15 questions were asked which considered all the aspects of creating a website such as the interface design, navigation, content and the users' reaction towards the system.

a) Descriptive Statistic

Statistical analysis, which is a descriptive statistic, is used in this study to describe and summarize the data that were collected from the test. The result of the acceptance test is shown in Figure 2 that detailed out the mean value for each of the questions.

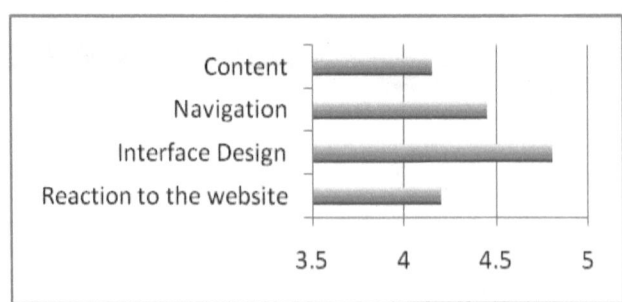

Figure2: Mean value for each aspect

All the mentioned aspects (reactions to the website, interface design, navigation and the content for developing a website) were measured using 5 Likert scale and the mean value for the entire questions are positive within a range between 3.70 and 5.From the result, it can be concluded that the recommender system is accepted by the users.

Conclusion and Recommendations

The web-based application, which is a website of Homestay Perlis, is a recommender system, which helps users to find the best homestay service in town. The study was developed by using Fuzzy Logic approach for TOPSIS method. The recommender system has been successfully developed and had received many positive responses from the users during the usability and user acceptance test. Apart from that, this system also gives a lot of benefits to tourism agencies as it able to suggest the best homestay besides promoting the culture, and the interesting places in Perlis. The result of the best recommended homestay is based on the review made by the users who experienced living in those homestays. Therefore, the result is always updated from time to time as the review continuously made by the users.

There are few recommendations suggested for the future work of the Homestay Perlis in order to improve its quality and features. For the future enhancement, the system is recommended to collaborate with the official website of those homestays so that the users will be able to make reservation directly from the website of Homestay Perlis. Besides that, more number of homestays can be added to the recommender system so that the users have more choices in selecting the best homestay service in Perlis. By enhancing the website of Homestay Perlis, all those recommendations may help this recommender system to be more useful in assisting the users in decision making.

References

Ahi, A., Aryanezhad, M.B., Ashtiani, B. &Makui, A. (2009). A novel approach to determine cell formation, intracellular machine layout and cell layout in the CMS problem based on TOPSIS method. *Journal in Computers and Operations Research*, Volume 36 Issue 5, 1478-1496.

Gaffney, G. (1999). *Information & Design.Designing for Human.* Retrieved January 7, 2016 from http://infodesign.com.au/usabilityresources/usabilitytesting/

Gunasekaran, N.& Anandkumarb, V. (2012). Factors of influence in choosing alternative accommodation:A study with reference to Pondicherry, a coastal heritage town. *Procedia – Social and Behavioral Sciences*, 1127-1132.

Hwang, C.L. & Yoon, K. (1981).*Multiple Attributes Decision Making: Methods and Applications.* Springer, Berlin Heidelberg.

Velasques, M. & Hester, P. (2013). An Analysis of Multi-Criteria Decision Making Methods. *International Journal of Operation Research*, 56-66.

Zadeh, L. (1975).The concept of a linguistic variable and its application to approximate reasoning. *Information Sciences* 8 (3), 199-249.

Zimmermann, H.J. (1991). *Fuzzy Set Theory and its Applications, (2ndedition).*Kluwer Academic Publishers, Boston, Dordrecht, London.

Article 13

A Glimpse of Malaysian Teachers' Reading Intervention Strategies for Children with Dyslexia

Aznoora Osman
Faculty of Computer & Mathematical Sciences
Universiti Teknologi MARA Cawangan Perlis

Wan Ahmad Jaafar Wan Yahaya, Aznan Che Ahmad
Centre for Instructional Technology & Multimedia
School of Educational Studies, Universiti Sains Malaysia

Abstract
This paper explores contemporary issues surrounding the teaching of reading towards dyslexic children in Malaysia. The objectives of the literature review and preliminary investigation were to ascertain the complexity of the issues, and to make informed decisions that warrant the development of educational app targeted for educators. It was discovered that children with dyslexia would normally experience distinctive learning difficulties than other children of learning disabilities. Nevertheless, the study revealed that most of them did not receive suitable classroom intervention. When teaching reading to these children, teachers should be aware of the major causes of their reading difficulties, and then employs strategies that could accommodate their personal strengths and weaknesses. Dyslexic children are often stigmatised and isolated by teachers and friends; therefore, it is vital to provide equal opportunity to learn for them. The result of this study calls for serious deliberation to train teachers about effective literacy intervention techniques that are precisely tailored for children with dyslexia.

Keywords: dyslexia, reading intervention, pre-service teachers, educational app

Introduction

Dyslexia is a specific language disorder that causes problem in reading, writing and speaking (Richardson, 1992). It has been described as a specific learning disability that is neurobiological in origin and is characterized by poor word recognition, spelling and decoding abilities despite having higher cognitive abilities and receiving effective classroom experience (Reid, Shaywitz & Shaywitz, 2003). Dyslexia is defined by the World Federation of Neurologist as "a disorder in children who, despite conventional classroom experience, fail to attain the language skills of reading, writing, and spelling commensurate with their intellectual abilities" (Gomez, 2004). In conjunction with this definition, the Malaysian Ministry of Education constitutes dyslexia as a condition in which a student experiences significant difficulties in reading, writing and/or spelling despite having a mental ability which is comparable to, or above those of average students (Zahrah, 2007; Kang, 2010). Children with dyslexia are described by Sheila and Samsilah (2006) as those who often have difficulties in retrieving the sound of alphabets, thus causing problems in spelling. In reading and writing, they often show transposition (eg: roli for lori; mali for lima), addition (eg: diyam for diam), omission (eg: buna for bunga) and letter reversals (eg: b for d).

Dyslexia within Malaysian Education System
In Malaysia, every child will normally start to learn recognizing alphabets, spelling and reading in the kindergarten as early as four years old. This will continue in primary school and by the age of seven or eight, they should be able to read and write at grade level. Unfortunately, there are many children who face difficulty in learning because it is estimated that in Malaysia, 50% of over 90000 pupils with learning difficulties are caused by dyslexia (Mohd. Fahmi, 2012). Rajesvari (2008) also discovered that there exist dyslexia-related difficulties among pupils in remedial classes. Strong evidence shows that children with dyslexia continue to experience reading problems into adolescence and adulthood (Shaywitz et al. 1999; Shaywitz, et al., 2003). Therefore, it is paramount to help dyslexic children to master the reading skills because if left untreated, they will develop low self-esteem and poor confidence (Zahrah, 2007). Furthermore, without effective intervention, a person could develop emotional problem because of inferiority and frustration (Wong, 2009).

Within Malaysian education system, dyslexia is positioned under special education, and categorized as a specific learning difficulty. In practice, after six months of schooling, Standard One pupils who are at risk of learning difficulties may be screened by their teachers using an instrument called *Instrumen Senarai Semak Disleksia* (Dyslexia Checklist Instrument) to check against dyslexia-related symptoms (Instrumen Senarai Semak Disleksia, 2011). The teachers will then recommend parents to have their children diagnosed by specialists at government hospitals. Upon diagnosis, these children must be registered with the Department of Welfare to acquire the *Orang Kurang Upaya, OKU* (People with Disabilities) card. This card would entitle them to enroll in the *Program Pendidikan Khas Integrasi Disleksia, PPKI Disleksia* (Dyslexia Special Education Integration Program, Dyslexia SEIP) and receive monthly financial allowance (Bahagian Pendidikan Khas, Kementerian Pelajaran Malaysia).

Dyslexia Learning Difficulties and Reading Intervention
Teaching individuals with dyslexia requires substantial understanding of their learning difficulties since the level of severity is different from one person to another (Rogers, 1991). Intervention needs to concentrate on individual's strengths and weaknesses, and have flexibility to adapt with the needs of the individual (An International Perspective on Dyslexia, 2007).

i. Multisensory technique
In order to help individuals with dyslexia in learning to read, they should be taught using multisensory technique that utilizes hearing, vision and touch (Wong, 2009). Training in phonological awareness is also essential to overcome their letter-shape-to-sound confusion (Spector, 1995; Thomson, 2010). The use of multisensory technique was found effective in helping at-risk children to memorize the shape of letters and to write them correctly (Nur Sharmimi, 2012). Rohaty, Mohd Anuar and Zahara (2012) also discovered that by using multisensory method for three months on dyslexic children who were attending remedial education classes, they had shown a significant increase in the ability to identify alphabets and words as well as in alphabet mastery. Therefore, it was recommended that multisensory technique be incorporated into literacy teaching toward dyslexic children to enhance their learning.

ii. Related Studies

The role of teachers is very important in helping these children to beat their literacy problem (Afendi, 2012), because they are often being laughed at in the classroom for making very simple mistake such as writing own name incorrectly, and consequently making them feeling socially isolated and having low self-esteem (Alfian, 2011). Rohaty and Shafie (2005) revealed that dyslexic children did not receive specific attention in general education as well as in special education; for example, these children were usually placed in remedial class along with other children who did not posses any dyslexia characteristics. Rohaty and Shafie (2005) also reported that some children with dyslexia, though having specific learning difficulty, were placed in general learning difficulties classes, which are a mix of various other learning difficulties such as autism, Down syndrome and slow learner. For that reason, they emphasized the urgent need to expose teachers to good teaching technique for dyslexics to improve the quality of education for this often neglected group of special needs children.

In another study, Liyana, Nurul and Khuzaiton (2013) discovered that most special education teachers in their case study did not possess sufficient knowledge about dyslexia symptoms, its associated difficulties and effective intervention technique; thus they did not know how to best help the dyslexic students in the special education class. Concerned with the situation, Liyana et al. (2013) advocated that children with dyslexia should be taught by teachers who are trained in the area. Likewise, Rohaty et al. (2012) insisted that teachers should receive specific training on dyslexia so that they could teach the children successfully.

In a nutshell, these previous studies upheld the need to improve the quality of education for dyslexic children and this could be achieved by enriching the pre-service university program of the special education teachers in dyslexia intervention.

iii. Courses in university for pre-service special education teachers

Pre-service teachers are the prospective teachers for special education schools, remedial classes and special education integration program at mainstream schools. Apparently, they are the ones who need to be exposed to examples of effective reading intervention technique for children with dyslexia. Nevertheless, based on the researchers' review of the syllabus in special education diploma and degree program of two public universities and one teacher training institute, the courses offered are mainly theory-intensive: (i) the introduction to learning difficulties and (ii) teaching strategy for individuals with learning difficulties. The introductory-level course exposes the pre-service teachers to all types of learning difficulties such as Down syndrome, autism, slow learner, cerebral palsy, dyslexia and attention deficit hyperactivity disorder (ADHD); just to name a few. Meanwhile, the latter discusses general topics in teaching individuals with any types of learning difficulties. Unfortunately, topic on the strategy of literacy intervention for individuals with dyslexia were noticeably missing, albeit their distinguished difficulties from other special need individuals. They require specific intervention that addresses the underlying cause of their reading problems, for example in matching letter-to-sound confusion. Ideally, the teaching technique employed by the teachers should be tailored to specifically address the pupils' difficulties in learning, as well as to accommodate to their current progress in reading (Zahrah, 2007).

Preliminary Investigations (PI)

The PI was conducted to investigate the current issues in the context of awareness of dyslexia and its intervention strategy. Semi-structured interview was chosen as the interview technique to create a semi-formal situation that is flexible and comfortable for the respondents whereby questions can be added or dropped freely and the researcher was able to adapt the level of language according to the language proficiency of the respondents (Chua, 2012). The semi-structured interviews were conducted with five special education teachers, two special education pre-service teachers, a headmaster of a school with Dyslexia SEIP classes and four parents of dyslexic children to gain information about their experience with the major topic of interest. The investigation also involved review of some researches and software for dyslexia intervention. The following sub sections will describe the results of the investigation.

i. Interview with special education teachers

Three primary school special education teachers were initially interviewed at their respective Dyslexia SEIP classes in three separate schools. The objectives of the interview were to gain information about the trainings related to dyslexia that the teachers receive during teacher preparation program and in-service, the teaching aids they use in classrooms and the teaching technique that they employ to help dyslexic children learn to read. It was discovered that all teachers did not receive formal training in dyslexia reading intervention during their pre-service training in university. There was no topic that focused on reading intervention for children with dyslexia. Therefore, they began learning about teaching strategy for pupils with dyslexia merely when they became teachers at the Dyslexia SEIP classes.

The interview was later conducted with another two secondary school special education teachers. They taught in special education classes at mainstream schools. The classes were attended by combination of students with various learning difficulties, including dyslexia. The teachers informed that they did not have adequate exposure towards dyslexia and its reading intervention technique. They confirmed that they had not undertaken any specific courses about dyslexia while studying in university. As such, they admitted that they had limited knowledge to help the present dyslexic students in their class and had used the same intervention technique for all students in the special education class.

They agreed that supplemental materials about reading intervention strategy would be beneficial to pre-service and in-service special education teachers, especially if it is accessible via computer software or the web. The interview revealed that there is a gap in the teacher preparatory program with regards to teaching dyslexic children.

ii. Interview with special education pre-service teachers

Pre-service teachers were selected as respondents in the PI because they are the future teachers for special education schools, remedial classes and special education integration program at mainstream schools. The interview was conducted with two special education pre-service teachers at a local university. The purpose was to find out the courses that they have undertaken with regards to dyslexia and their opinion about teaching children with dyslexia. Both of them informed that they have learned an introductory course about learning difficulties and will learn in the coming semester about general teaching strategies towards children with learning difficulties; however, they were uncertain about effective strategy in teaching children with dyslexia to read.

iii. Interview with headmaster

The headmaster of a school with Dyslexia SEIP class revealed that there was no specific strategy being employed by the teachers in order to overcome reading difficulties among pupils with dyslexia, since the problems vary from one child to another. Therefore, the idea of developing a multimedia learning application to persuade teachers in learning about intervention strategies for dyslexic individuals were highly welcomed. The headmaster added that the learning application should not only be used for training of pre-service teachers, but also for in-service teachers.

iv. Interview with parents of dyslexic children

Four mothers were interviewed. Their children were learning either under the Dyslexia SEIP class or remedial class. They themselves wanted to know how to best support their children socially and emotionally since they realized that these children have very low self-esteem and confidence, due to the maltreatment they receive from some teachers and friends. They had high hope that teachers could be well trained with knowledge and skills in teaching pupils with difficulties to read.

v. Review on research and software for dyslexia intervention
Past literature focused on using computer based materials, especially educational multimedia to remedy reading difficulties among dyslexic children. These products were developed as reading aid using Malay language and the target users were the dyslexic children themselves. For instance, a courseware named MyLexics (Muhammad Haziq, Syariffanor & Shahril, 2009) were developed to be used as reading and writing aid by dyslexic children. Other examples of courseware are the X-Leksia (Anusuria, Umawathy, Zeratul & Mohd Hafiz, 2007) which is a reading aid in Malay language for pre-schoolers, E-Z-Disleksia (Siti Salwa, Rozita, Eze Manzura, Karimah & Mohd Zaliman, 2010) which is a reading aid in Malay language for dyslexics who are in early stage of reading and FonicsTutor (Noor Eszereen, 2011).

On the other hand, there is a web-based system created and owned by the School of Educational Studies in Universiti Sains Malaysia (USM), called the e-PKhas. It is a portal where anyone could register and log-in to view and download the resources for teaching and learning in special education. The information caters for dyslexia, remedial class, learning difficulties, and hearing and visual impairment. Nevertheless, there is no specific topic that concentrates on the step-by-step strategies to help improve reading skill for children with dyslexia. As of the completion of the PI, there was no reported literature on training software for teachers about dyslexia reading intervention.

Conclusion
In summary, the PI has shown that there exists a gap in the context of teaching children with dyslexia. There is lack of concentration on intervention strategies that is adaptive to the causative factors of reading difficulties among dyslexic children. Therefore, it is crucial to provide the right help and intervention for children with dyslexia as early as possible so that they could

lead a normal life and safeguard their well-being. Most previous research developed educational products to be used by the dyslexic children; however, none of those has utilized the educational multimedia technology to enhance knowledge of teachers in teaching these children. Hence, there is an opportunity to fill the gap in the enhancement of special education teachers' skills, especially in producing supplemental materials that could be used as a reference tool beyond lectures and training courses.

References

Afendi, A. B. (2012). *Mengatasi Kelemahan Menulis Huruf Terbalik Menggunakan Buku Garis Tiga Dan Kaedah Pengulangan Bimbingan Individu*. Paper presented at the Seminar Penyelidikan Tindakan IPG Kampus Batu Lintang, Sarawak, 27-28 Sept, 2012.

Alfian, M. (2011). Teknik "smart cilik" bagi mengatasi masalah struktur penulisan murid simptom disleksia visual. Paper presented at the *Seminar Penyelidikan dan Pembangunan Inovasi Pendidikan*, Pahang, 2011.

Anusuria, D., Umawathy, T., Zeratul, I.M.Y. & Mohd Hafiz, Z. (2007). *X-Leksia: Creation, Assessment and Implementation*. Proceeding of Int'l Conference on Teaching and Learning (ICTL2007), Putrajaya, Malaysia.

An International Perspective on Dyslexia. (2007, Dec). *Literacy Today*(53), 26-27.

Bahagian Pendidikan Khas, Kementerian Pelajaran Malaysia. Retrieved from http://www.moe.gov.my/v/BPKhas

Chua, Y. P. (2012). *Mastering Research Methods*. Kuala Lumpur: McGraw-Hill.

Gomez, C. (2004). Dyslexia in Malaysia. In I. e. a. E. Smythe (Eds.), International Book of Dyslexia: A Guide to Practice and Resources.Retrieved on Oct 10, 2011 from http://www.wiley.com/legacy/wileychi/dyslexia/supp/Malaysia.pdf

Instrumen Senarai Semak Disleksia (2011). Jabatan Pendidikan Khas. Putrajaya:Kementerian Pelajaran Malaysia.

Kang, S. C. (Sept 26, 2010). Taking the lid off learning disorders. *The StarOnline*. Retrieved on Nov 10, 2011 from http://thestar.com.my/education/story.asp?file=/2010/9/26/education/7094 528&sec=education

Liyana, A., Nurul, F.H., & Khuzaiton, Z. (2013). *Persepsi dan pengalaman guru pendidikan khas dalam menghadapi permasalahan disleksia dalam kemahiran literasi*. Paper presented at Seminar Sains Kemanusiaan OKU Peringkat Kebangsaan 2013, Kota Bharu, Kelantan. Retrieved on April 4, 2013 from http://umkeprints.umk.edu.my/2328/

Mohd. Fahmi, M.Y. (Mac 24, 2012). 45,000 budak hidap Disleksia. *Berita Harian Online*. Retrieved on Aug 5, 2012 from www.bharian.com.my/bharian/articles/45_000budakhidapDisleksia

Muhammad Haziq, L.A., Syariffanor, H.,&Shahril, P. (2009). MyLexics: an assistive courseware for dyslexic children to learn basic Malay language. *ACM SIGACCESS Accessibility and Computing*(95), 3-9.

Noor Eszereen, J. (2011). *UPM cipta perisian untuk kanak- kanak disleksia*.Retrieved on Dec 14, 2011 from Universiti Putra Malaysia Institutional Repository. http://psasir.upm.edu.my/17758/1/UPM_Cipta_Perisian_Fonik_Tutor_untuk_Kanak-kanak_Disleksia.pdf

Nur Sharmimi, B. (2012). *Kaedah VAKT dan menulis nama*. Paper presented at the Seminar Penyelidikan Tindakan IPG Kampus Batu Lintang, Sept 27-28, 2012, Sarawak, Malaysia.

Rajesvari, R. (2008). *Masalah Disleksia Dalam Kalangan Murid-Murid Pemulihan Di Sekolah Rendah, Pulau Pinang*.(Unpublished Master Thesis). Universiti Sains Malaysia, Pulau Pinang.

Rohaty, M. & Shafie, M.N. (2005). Simptom Disleksia Kanak-kanak Prasekolah. *Jurnal Pendidikan 30*, 3 - 19.

Rohaty, M., Mohd Anuar, A., & Zahara, Z. (2012). Effects of a Multisensory Programme on Dyslexic Students: Identification and Mastery of the Alphabet. *Research Journal of Applied Sciences, 7*(7), 340-343.

Reid, L., Shaywitz, S., & Shaywitz, B. (2003). Defining dyslexia, comorbidity, teachers' knowledge of language and reading. *Annals of Dyslexia, 53*, 1-14.

Richardson, S. O. (1992). Historical Perspectives on Dyslexia. *Journal of Learning Disabilities, 25*(1), 40-47.

Rogers, T. (1991). Dyslexia: A Survivor's Story. *Journal of Learning Disabilities, 24*(2), 121-123.

Shaywitz, S. E., Fletcher, J. M., Holahan, J. M., Shneider, A. E., Marchione, K. E., Stuebing, K. K. (1999). Persistence of dyslexia: The Connecticut longitudinal study at adolescence. *Pediatrics, 104*(6), 1351-1359.

Shaywitz, S. E., Shaywitz, B. A., Fulbright, R. K., Skudlarski, P., Mencl, W. E., Constable, R. T., et al. (2003). Neural systems for compensation and persistence: young adult outcome of childhood reading disability. *Biological psychiatry, 54*(1), 25-33.

Sheila, D. &Samsilah, R. (2006). *Apa Itu Disleksia? Panduan untuk ibubapa, guru dan kaunselor*. Selangor: PTS Professional Publishing.

Siti Salwa, I., Rozita, I., Eze Manzura, M.M., Karimah, U., & Mohd Zaliman, M.Y. (2010). EZ-Disleksia for Dyslexic Children. Proceedings of Regional Conference on Knowledge Integration in ICT (June 1-2, 2010). Putrajaya, Malaysia.

Spector, J. E. (1995). Phonemic awareness training: Application of principles of direct instruction. *Reading & Writing Quarterly: Overcoming Learning Difficulties, 11*(1), 37-51.

Thomson, J. (2010). *Good Practice in interventions for teaching dyslexic learners and in teacher training in English speaking countries.*Harvard Graduate School of Education. Retrieved on May 20, 2013 from http://www.dyslexia-international.org/WDF/Files/WDF2010-Thomson-Report.pdf

Wong, L. Z. (2009). Hope for dyslexics. *The StarOnline*. Retrieved from http://thestar.com.my/lifestyle/story.asp?file=/2009/3/16/lifefocus/333634 8&sec=lifefocus

Zahrah, A. (2007). Murid Disleksia Belajar Mengeja Dengan Melakar/Melukis Gambar. Paper presented at Persidangan Kebangsaan Guru Cemerlang Malaysia 2007, 3-6 Sept 2007, Johor Baharu.

Article 14

A Preliminary Investigation: Feasibility of an Interactive Multimedia Application in Increasing Knowledge and Awareness of Cyber Bullying Among Adolescents

Nadia Abdul Wahab
Faculty of Computer & Mathematical Sciences
Universiti Teknologi MARA Cawangan Perlis

Wan Ahmad Jaafar Wan Yahaya
Centre for Instructional Technology & Multimedia
School of Educational Studies, Universiti Sains Malaysia

Abstract
This paper describes a preliminary investigation of how the capabilities of an interactive multimedia application may be used to raise understanding and awareness towards cyber bullying among adolescents. Nine respondents were selected to participate in the interview ranging from three parents, three primary school students and three Secondary school students from Kedah and Perlis state of Malaysia. The findings of the interviews and literature reviews confirm that there is a lack of knowledge and awareness that needs to be addressed among adolescents especially in Malaysia. The paper also concludes that an interactive multimedia application needs to be designed and developed to increase knowledge and awareness on cyber-bullying among adolescents.
Keywords: cyber bullying, preliminary investigation, interactive multimedia

Introduction

The issue of bullying has long been a topic of discussion amongst educationists, academicians and researchers. Bully causes individuals to feel hurt, pain, embarrassment, fear, loneliness, isolation and sadness. Bullying is not limited merely to physical conduct like beating, kicking, pinching or pushing someone. Bullying also exists in other forms as in speech, by calling someone names, cruel jokes, threatening or slandering. Now, there is a new channel though which someone is bullied, and that is through the Internet and other ICT devices like smart phones. This form of bullying is known as cyber bullying. Willard (2005) defined cyber bullying as sending or posting harmful texts or images through the use of digital communication devices.

Like traditional bullying, cyber bullying victims are also exposed to the negative consequences of this phenomenon. They might isolate themselves especially from school activities, become stressed, and possibly contemplate suicide (Willard, 2005). Victims of bullying are usually afraid of complaining to adults about the incidents that have befallen them. This is because they are concerned that they may be forbidden to access the Internet and that they may not be allowed to use smart phones and computers after the complaint is made. In contrast to traditional bullying which usually occurs in schools, cyber bullying frequently occurs at home. This causes the affected individual to feel that there is nowhere else that they can seek refuge at (Wolak & Mitchell, 2000).

Multimedia offers exciting possibilities for meeting the needs of the new generation learners. Neo and Neo (2001) defined multimedia as "the combination of various digital media types, such as text, images, sound, and video, into an integrated multisensory interactive application or presentation to convey a message or information to an audience." In multimedia learning, the delivery of instructional include visual and auditory information and learners use of this information to construct knowledge. According to Mayer (2001), people learn better from words and pictures than from words alone. In this perspective, words include written and spoken text, and pictures include static graphic images, animation and video, or in other word, multimedia.

Findings
Literature review and preliminary investigation were conducted in order to gain in-depth understanding on the current situation of cyber-bullying and the need to raise the knowledge and awareness of this phenomenon among adolescents. The findings of these activities will be discussed in the next sub-section.

i. Literature Review
Literature review was conducted in order to understand the current situation of cyber-bullying among adolescents in Malaysia and to investigate the technologies being designed, developed and used for cyber bullying intervention.

a) Cyber-bullying and adolescents
With the advances in technology, most adolescents use Internet technology to create social relationships through social websites such as Facebook, Twitter, Friendster, etc that offer interesting and enjoyable functions. It cannot be denied that social websites such as these have many plus points and advantages such as the ability to connect and discuss current issues in cyber space. Nevertheless there are also disadvantages as its usage is without control (Willard, 2007).

Generally, adolescents today are knowledgeable about computer technology but they are not mature enough to understand the implications of their online activities and as a result, many adolescents are caught in unhealthy activities and social problems within the cyber world, such as cyber-bullying (Guan and Subrahmanyam, 2009). There are various negative effects resulting from cyber bullying. These include the possibility of someone facing psychological function deficiency and other problems such as being anti-social, anxiety disorder and depressive symptoms (Cappadocia, 2008; Tynes and Giang, 2009; Wolak, et. al, 2007).

Most victims of cyber-bullying are frequently distracted, feel low esteem and have a tendency to commit suicide (Patchin & Hinduja, 2006). A study on cyber-bullying amongst adolescents found that 33% of the respondents admitted that they were victims of cyber-bullying, while 22% of adolescents felt sadness and wished to commit suicide as a result of cyber-bullying (Patchin and Hinduja, 2006).

A study by Beran and Li (2005) found that victim of cyber-bullying were less likely to attend school, could not concentrate on their school-work, and received lower grades than students who were not bullied. Beran and Li (2005) also found that victims of cyber-bullying experienced feelings of anger and sadness. According to a study conducted by Patchin and Hinduja (2010), both victims and offenders of cyber-bullying have significantly lower self-esteem than those who had little or no experience with cyber-bullying.

From the above studies, it can be concluded that cyber-bullying can leave enormously negative impact on the public generally and on adolescents specifically. Therefore appropriate measures should be taken to curb this menace. Developing an interactive multimedia application that is able to provide knowledge and awareness to adolescents is one of a measure that can be taken to overcome this problem.

b) Cyber-bullying in Malaysia

In Malaysia, cyber bullying cases that are becoming more rampant in schools pose a new challenge for educationists and parents. The Deputy Minister of Education was reported saying that the spread of false information, written texts that demean, degrade and threaten through the short messaging system (SMS) and Internet as well as video recordings that are circulated amongst students can have emotional consequences in victims. Cyber bullying may be a new disciplinary problem in this country but it has long been widespread amongst students in Western countries that have caused mental anguish. It has lasting consequences on victims when faced with such overwhelming stress (Dahari, 2008).

A Head of Business for Norton South-east Asia, was reported saying that cyber bullying are generally perpetrated by adolescent boys or girls, and troubled adults who harass, scare and embarrass others through SMS, e-mail, short messages in chat rooms, social networks and websites, including online gaming. He says that even though this phenomenon is not as serious as it is abroad, nevertheless, the advent of social bullying has started as more and more adolescents and adults misuse telecommunication technology for their own satisfaction by channeling their anger through this medium (Alias, 2010).

Research carried out by Norton Online Family has found that children in Malaysia spend an average of 19 hours a week browsing the Internet. It all happens after exposure to technological games and gadgets like laptops, iPads, iPods as well as a variety of smart phones like the iPhone and Blackberry. We should not, however, lay the blame squarely on the children. This exposure has resulted from parents who, instead of giving their children the attention the children are seeking from them, give them those highly advanced technological "toys"(Halid, 2011).

c) Technologies being used for cyber-bullying intervention
Beside formal prevention programs being conducted in schools, there are several technologies put forth throughout the world to deal with the issue of cyber bullying (Table 1). Most of the existing applications usually emphasize the dissemination of information concerning cyber bullying to the general public through websites and portals. There are also several applications developed for children and teenagers that guide on how to deal with cyber bullying.

Table 1: The Different Type of Technologies Being Used For Cyber Bullying

Technology	Sources	Description
Website/ portal	Cyberbullying.us Cyberbullying.org	• These websites gives information about cyber-bullying and provides options for getting help. • Focusing on establishing understanding and awareness among children. • Contents of these websites are rather static and contain more text compared to other multimedia elements • Could be less attractive for adolescents

Game based application	Alex Wonder Kid Cyberdetective	• This game application was designed to educate students in grades 4-8 regarding cyber-bullying. • Focusing on how children could stay safer online and avoid cyber bullies. • Information about cyber-bullying is quite limited
Multimedia / animation	BrainPOP educational animated movie on cyber-bullying	• Emphasize on security issues and prevention of cyber-bullying. • Focusing on creating understanding and awareness on cyber-bullying • Crucial information such as examples of cyber-bullying behaviour needs to be included
	Chris Webster's cyber-bullying page	• Using simple animation in an interactive website • Give general information on cyber-bullying to the communities • The graphics used are not really appealing and quite confusing. • The information that is given about cyber-bullying is rather limited.
Virtual Reality/ Simulation	Cyberbullying Virtual Scenarios	• Using SecondLife, an online virtual world to create scenarios and simulations of cyber-bullying incidents and how to deal with it. • Aims to give information on coping strategy. • Important sub-topics such cyber-bullying behavior are not included.

Even though there are few technologies that have been developed specifically to provide knowledge and awareness on the topic of cyber-bullying, nevertheless, there are still several flaws, especially from the aspect of content and presentation of the applications. This underlines the need for the development of a multimedia application that is more comprehensive and interesting that is appropriate within the context of adolescents in Malaysia. This situation motivated the researcher to develop a multimedia application in Bahasa Malaysia to provide knowledge and awareness about cyber-bullying specifically for the adolescents in this country.

ii. Preliminary Investigation

The researcher had conducted a Preliminary Investigation (PI) to gain in-depth understanding of cyber-bullying issue among adolescents in Malaysia. Unstructured interview technique has been chosen to investigate the current level of knowledge and awareness of cyber bullying among adolescents and the prevention programs that have been implemented in schools. During the PI, the researcher interviewed a cyber-bullying expert, five secondary school students and three parents to gain in-depth understanding regarding this issue.

a) Interview with cyber-bullying expert

The researcher had interviewed a senior lecturer from a public university who is also an expert in cyber-bullying. According to him, knowledge and awareness about cyber-bullying amongst adolescents in this country is still at a low level. His opinion is in tandem with the results of the Microsoft Global Youth Online Behavior Survey which found that knowledge and awareness about cyber-bullying was below average in Malaysia (*Microsoft Global Youth Online Behavior Survey*, 2012).

With more than five years' experience in studying this phenomenon, the expert stated that cyber-bullying had become more serious recently and was a global threat that must be addressed. Cyber-bullying does not only happen abroad, it is also escalating in Malaysia. Furthermore, according to this expert, the group that is most vulnerable to this threat is adolescents.

The expert added that most adolescents have not been exposed to what cyber-bullying actually means, for example, the acts of cyber-bullying and its dangers. They are also clueless on how to deal with and eradicate it. This expert also opined that adolescents would normally not report it to their parents, school or the relevant authorities if they were being bullied online or if they knew of a friend who is being bullied. They are more inclined to keep it to themselves or to tell their closest friends.

b) Interviews with adolescents
The researcher had the opportunity to carry out an unstructured interview with five secondary school students to validate the research problem. The participants comprise three girls and two boys aged between 13 and 16 years. All of them have Internet access at home. All five participants own a Facebook and Instagram account, at least one email account and smart phones. Two of them also own Twitter accounts. All are familiar with WhatsApp, WeChat and SMS services. One is also an active blogger.

These five adolescents revealed that almost all their classmates have Facebook, Instagram, WhatsApp, WeChat and email accounts and several have their own web blogs. All of them agreed that the applications most frequently used to communicate with their friends are the WhatsApp and WeChat, followed by Facebook, Instagram, SMS and emails. These students have also been found to have used the messaging application on Facebook to chat with their friends. They also read and are followers of their friends' web blogs.

Despite admitting that the communication technology that they use is extremely beneficial in helping them to communicate with friends and teachers, all five students did not deny that there are unhealthy elements within the virtual world. These adolescents also revealed that social networking sites such as Facebook and

Twitter have been wrongly used to spread slander and inaccurate information, to criticise friends, gossip and argue.

When asked about cyber bullying, all five students admitted that they were not certain of what is meant by "cyber-bullying" exactly or its characteristics. Three students have also not gained exposure to cyber-bullying before this, neither through their parents, teachers, readings or the mass media. Two students stated that while they had heard of cyber-bullying, they did not fully understand this issue. They did not consider cyber-bullying to be very serious nor did they think that it could seriously endanger adolescents.

After being given an explanation about the definition and characteristics of cyber-bullying, all of the students admitted that they had been involved with this phenomenon, or at least know of friends that cyber bullied or have been cyber bullied. One boy who had bullied admitted that he has, on several occasions, criticised a classmate on the Facebook. Using the flaming method, the boy has the intention of making fun of that friend. Nevertheless, he did not think that his actions were acts of cyber-bullying.

A girl admitted that she had circulated emails that revealed the secrets of someone who had been a close friend to her school mates. This happened because she wanted to get back at being bullied by that friend whereby that friend had spread gossip about her on the Facebook. This accident could be associated with outing and trickery method of cyber-bullying. Other than the actions stated above, the three adolescents revealed that they had heard and known of friends who had been cyber bullied through acts like slandering, spreading untrue stories, hacked accounts and such.

When asked about what action they had taken after they had been bullied or what action they would take if they were bullied in the future, four students said that if the incidents were not serious, they would not complain to their parents or teachers. They would instead feel more at ease sharing the experience with their peers. Three of the adolescents revealed that their parents rarely monitored their online activities for example, finding out which websites they were browsing and the contents of what had been posted on the Facebook. Only two of the five students admitted occasional monitoring by parents but one of them had removed the mother from the "Friend" list on Facebook to keep the parents from finding out about their online activities and also out of concern that the parents would not allow further Internet access.

c) Interviews with parents

At this preliminary investigation phase, the researcher held an interview session with two mothers and a father. They were parents of secondary school students from a school in Perlis. When the matter of cyber-bullying was introduced, all three did not appear to fully grasp the concept whereby two of the parents revealed that they had never had any exposure to it before this. The other parent had heard about cyber-bullying but had not been too concerned about it before the interview.

Two of the three respondents admitted that they rarely monitored their children's online activities due to work commitments and time constraints. They were uncertain if their children had ever been cyber bullied or not. One of the parents said that even with constant monitoring on online activities, there had never been any discussions with the children concerning safety and privacy as well as bullying in the virtual world.

After being given an explanation about the definition and characteristics of cyber-bullying behaviour, all three parents agreed that their children might probably have been or will be involved with this phenomenon if they were not monitored. All the parents were of the opinion that the problem of cyber-bullying is a serious problem that could distract their children's attention from learning as well as have negative consequences on their children's psychological growth.

Discussion and Conclusion

As a result of the preliminary investigation, it may be concluded that cyber-bullying clearly is present in our society of late especially amongst adolescents. Nevertheless, the understanding and awareness of the adolescents regarding this issue is still at a very low level. The effort to increase understanding and awareness should be extended to all levels of society especially amongst adolescents and several methods and efforts should be taken.

Other than creating awareness through seminars, talks and the mass media, awareness can also be heightened through the use of appropriate technology and tools. Although there are few technologies that have been developed specifically to provide knowledge and awareness on the topic of cyber-bullying, nevertheless, there are still several flaws, especially from the aspect of content and presentation of the applications. With today's technology, an interactive multimedia application would be an appropriate medium to instill knowledge and awareness amongst adolescents concerning the ever-growing menace of cyber-bullying.

References

Alias, C. W. B. (2010-05-08, 08 May 2010). Bahana pembuli siber. *Berita Harian*.

Beran, T., & Li, Q. (2005). Cyber-harassment: A study of a new method for an old behavior. *journal of educational Computing Research, 32*(3), 265-277.

Cappadocia, M. C. (2008). *Cyberbullying and Cybervictimization: Prevalence, Stability, Risk and Protective Factors, and Psychosocial Problems*: York University.

Dahari, R. M. (2008-05-05). Buli siber cabaran baru di sekolah. *Utusan Malaysia*.

Guan, S. S., & Subrahmanyam, K. (2009). Youth Internet use: risks and opportunities. *Curr Opin Psychiatry, 22*(4), 351-356.

Microsoft Global Youth Online Behavior Survey. (2012). Microsoft Corporation.

Neo, M. N. T. K. (2001). Innovative teaching: Using multimedia in a problem based learning environment. *Educational Technology & Society, 4*(4).

Patchin, J. W., & Hinduja, S. (2006). Bullies move beyond the schoolyard a preliminary look at cyberbullying. *Youth violence and juvenile justice, 4*(2), 148-169.

Patchin, J. W., & Hinduja, S. (2010). Cyberbullying and Self Esteem. *Journal of School Health, 80*(12), 614-621.

Tynes, B., & Giang, M. (2009). *Online victimization, depression and anxiety among adolescents in the US.* Paper presented at the European Psychiatry.

Willard, N. (2005). Educator's Guide to Cyberbullying Addressing the Harm Caused by Online Social Cruelty. Retrieved July, 26, 2012, from http://www.asdk12.org/middlelink/avb/bully_topics/educatorsguide_c yberbullying.pdf

Willard, N. E. (2007). *Cyber-safe kids, cyber-savvy teens : helping young people learn to use the internet safely and responsibly*: San Francisco, Calif. : Jossey-Bass, c2007 (Norwood, Mass. : Books24x7.com).

Wolak, J., & Mitchell, K. (2000). Youth Internet Saftey Survey. from http://www.unh.edu/ccrc/projects/internet_survey.html

Wolak, J., Mitchell, K. J., & Finkelhor, D. (2007). Does online harassment constitute bullying? An exploration of online harassment by known peers and online-only contacts. *J Adolesc Health, 41*(6 Suppl 1), S51-58.

www.ingramcontent.com/pod-product-compliance
Lightning Source LLC
Chambersburg PA
CBHW032026170526
45157CB00002B/869